Measuring and Managing
Employee Performance

FINANCIAL TIMES
Prentice Hall

In an increasingly competitive world, it is quality of thinking that gives an edge – an idea that opens new doors, a technique that solves a problem, or an insight that simply helps make sense of it all.

We work with leading authors in the fields of management and finance to bring cutting-edge thinking and best learning practice to a global market.

Under a range of leading imprints, including *Financial Times Prentice Hall*, we create world-class print publications and electronic products giving readers knowledge and understanding which can then be applied, whether studying or at work.

To find out more about our business and professional products, you can visit us at www.business-minds.com

For other Pearson Education publications, visit www.pearsoned-ema.com

Pearson Education

MANAGEMENT BRIEFINGS
HUMAN RESOURCES

Measuring and Managing Employee Performance

A practical manual to maximise organisational performance through people

PAUL KEARNS

HR-EXPERT
www.hr-expert.com

FINANCIAL TIMES
Prentice Hall
An imprint of Pearson Education

London	New York	San Francisco	Toronto	Sydney
Tokyo	Singapore	Hong Kong	Cape Town	Madrid
Paris	Milan	Munich	Amsterdam	

PEARSON EDUCATION LIMITED

Head Office:
Edinburgh Gate
Harlow CM20 2JE
Tel: +44 (0)1279 623623
Fax: +44 (0)1279 431059

London Office:
128 Long Acre
London WC2E 9AN
Tel: +44 (0)20 7447 2000
Fax: +44 (0)20 7240 5771
Website: www.hr-expert.com

First published in Great Britain in 2000

© Paul Kearns 2000

The right of Paul Kearns to be identified as Author
of this Work has been asserted by him in accordance
with the Copyright, Designs and Patents Act 1988.

ISBN 0 273 64998 1

British Library Cataloguing in Publication Data
A CIP catalogue record for this book can be obtained from the British Library.

All rights reserved; no part of this publication may be reproduced, stored
in a retrieval system, or transmitted in any form or by any means, electronic,
mechanical, photocopying, recording, or otherwise without either the prior
written permission of the Publishers or a licence permitting restricted copying
in the United Kingdom issued by the Copyright Licensing Agency Ltd,
90 Tottenham Court Road, London W1P 0LP. This book may not be lent,
resold, hired out or otherwise disposed of by way of trade in any form
of binding or cover other than that in which it is published, without the
prior consent of the Publishers.

10 9 8 7 6 5 4 3 2 1

Typeset by Boyd Elliott Typesetting
Printed and bound in Great Britain

The Publishers' policy is to use paper manufactured from sustainable forests.

About the author

Paul Kearns is Senior Partner at the Personnel Works Partnership and is widely recognised as a leading authority in the field of employee performance measurement. His ground-breaking methodology is extensively used in many major blue-chip companies and public sector organisations.

He is a thought-provoking conference speaker on the subjects of HR strategy, measurement and evaluation and is a visiting MBA lecturer at Cranfield University. His work and reputation have also been recognised by the highly prestigious Judge Institute of Management at Cambridge, where he was invited to present an original paper at their 1998 International Conference on 'Performance Measurement – Theory and Practice'.

Many of the practical tools which he has developed are economically and lucidly explained in two previous titles in this series *Measuring HR and the Impact on the Bottom Line* (1995) and with Tony Miller *Measuring the Impact of Training and Development on the Bottom Line* (1996).

As an outspoken critic of modern management fads and fashions Paul prefers pragmatic solutions to complex business problems. He firmly believes that all business issues can be addressed in a simple, 'down-to-earth' way, but he has found this common-sense approach to be so rare that he now refers to it as 'leading-edge common sense'!

Paul can be contacted at:

Personnel Works
PO Box 109
Bristol
BS9 4DH
UK

Phone: (+0044) 117 9146984
Email: pkearns@breathemail.net

Dedication

This book is dedicated to all those who would rather choose a common-sense solution in preference to what their boss just told them to do, to what the latest management fad suggests and certainly to what the management accounts department wants.

Contents

Preface — xi

PART 1 THE GROUNDWORK – THE PRINCIPLES OF EMPLOYEE PERFORMANCE MEASUREMENT — 1

1 Why the need for yet another book on performance measurement — 3
- Not all management books are the same — 6
- Are the latest management texts saying anything new? — 6
- Do the people who buy management books read them? — 7

2 Understanding, measurement and learning — 9
- Do you understand? — 11
- Kearns' seven levels of understanding — 14
- You know you have learned something useful when you get a result — 15
- Do the latest management ideas get results? — 16
- The perennial subject of measurement — 17
- The PDCA cycle is a cycle of performance and learning — 20

3 We measure everything but we're not very good at it — 23
- We measure everything but we're not very good at it — 25
- The principles of employee performance measurement — 26
- A definition of employee performance measurement — 28
- Data, performance information and other terminology — 29

4 Revisiting performance measurement — 31
- Why performance measurement needs to change — 33
- How performance measurement needs to change — 36
- The balanced business scorecard in practice — 38

PART 2 HOW TO DO IT – THE TRICKS OF THE TRADE 41

5 But I don't want to be measured 43
The psychological contract 45
Resistance to measurement 46
The positive side of measurement 47

6 Management information systems and people performance 53
Management information systems 55
Where are we now? 56
Measurement tips – using measurement intelligently 59

7 The performance measurement proposition 63
The performance measurement curve 65
Managing underperformance 67
Acceptable performers 69
Superior performers 69
Starting to produce the performance distribution curve 70
Different curves for different aspects of performance 70
Equal opportunities for maximum added value 71
Six key elements to maximise individual performance and added value 73
Installing an employee performance measurement and management system 76

8 Performance and added value are not the same 81
What is added value? 83
Double-Glazing 'R' Us 85

9 Motivation and performance – what's the connection? 89
Does high morale lead to high productivity? 92

10 Rewarding performance 95
Paying for performance 97
Establishing base pay levels 98

	Performance related pay (PRP)	99
	Fat cats and market rates	100

11 Performance appraisal and assessment — 103

Basic or minimum standard activity	105
Critical activity and risk	105
Added value activities	106
ROI	106
Non-added value activity	108
Performance measures hidden in the business plan	109
When and how often should performance be assessed?	110

12 Key people – critical performance — 113

Spotting key people	115
Developing key people	116
Succession planning	117
Retaining key people	118

PART 3 THE STRATEGIC PERSPECTIVE – DEVELOPING AN EMPLOYEE PERFORMANCE CULTURE — 119

13 A strategic perspective on performance measurement — 121

Hurdles towards high performance	123

14 How structure and process affect performance — 129

Structural change	132
Process change	133
Simultaneous structure and process change	135
Matrix organisations	135
The office equipment company	136
Five phases of performance improvement through process redesign	139

15 Connecting performance, knowledge management, and human and intellectual capital — 141

If that is the answer – what was the question again?	143
Putting people on the balance sheet	144

There is 'performance' and then there is *performance*   145
Performance and innovation   146
Knowledge management and performance   147

16 The role of human resource management in performance measurement and management   149

HR strategy and performance   151
Why traditional appraisal schemes don't work   152
The advent of performance management systems   153
Why the personnel function needs to change   154
The HR function as performance management function   155
The need for a specialist performance measurement and management unit   155
Training in performance measurement   156

Appendix: Employee performance measurement and management tools   157

Tool 1: Where are you in employee performance measurement – a primer   159
Tool 2: Producing an employee performance distribution curve   160
Tool 3: Using the distribution curve to improve performance   161
Tool 4: Establishing what factors contribute to improved individual performance   163
Tool 5: Does motivation influence performance?   164
Tool 6: Creating a closed loop feedback system   167
Tool 7: How to set performance objectives   169
Tool 8: Personal added value and performance review (PAVPR)   172
Tool 9: Which of your activities add the most value?   174
Tool 10: Spot the performance and added value measures   176
Tool 11: Performance trend chart   177
Tool 12: Redesigning the organisation to improve performance   178
Tool 13: Checking levels of understanding   181

References   183

Preface

This book is an attempt to provide some simple, workable answers to most, if not all, of the questions I have ever been asked on employee performance measurement and management. If you think the answers are too simple then consider how successful any attempt at greater sophistication might prove to be.

The concepts, ideas, tools and techniques presented here have been developed over the last decade on a very tough test pad. They have been tried out in a wide range of organisations, both commercial and public sector. In addition, they have been bounced off hundreds of participants on the public conferences, seminars and workshops that I run. The ideas that have made it into this book are those that survived all of the questions, criticism and resistance thrown at them by the disbelieving and cynical. You will not come across the ones that did not stand up to this rigorous test; they have been binned.

This book not only looks at the specifics of employee performance measurement but also the context in which we have to apply it. There is no point in trying to teach someone how to fish without spending some time considering the variety of factors that come into play, such as currents, shallows and the weather. The organisational environment has a very important part to play in performance measurement.

Finally, the terms performance measurement and performance management will be used liberally throughout. They are not synonymous but you cannot have management without measurement and there is not much point having measurement for the sake of it. The two should always be seen as totally interdependent.

Part 1

The groundwork – the principles of employee performance measurement

- 1 Why the need for yet another book on performance measurement 3
- 2 Understanding, measurement and learning 9
- 3 We measure everything but we're not very good at it 23
- 4 Revisiting performance measurement 31

Why the need for yet another book on performance measurement

- Not all management books are the same 6
- Are the latest management texts saying anything new? 6
- Do the people who buy management books read them? 7

Why the need for yet another book

A search on Amazon.com at the time of writing this in September 1999, using the keywords 'performance measurement' produced 70 matches. Using the keywords 'business performance measurement' produced 29. The key words 'employee performance measurement' did not produce any matches. Is this because there is no interest in the specific subject of employee performance measurement or is it because it is still a very new subject?

My guess is that it is a combination of lack of interest and difficulty. The lack of interest is probably because most organisations think they already measure employee performance well. Also, managing employees is not everyone's favourite pastime. If you asked any chief executive officer (CEO) how they were planning to achieve a significant competitive advantage or other major improvement in their business, I wonder what their first reaction would be? Assuming they are not too busy just surviving, would it be to develop lots of new products as soon as possible? Or a major investment in new equipment, the latest technology or perhaps e-commerce? How about a drive for global expansion or yet another cost reduction programme? Maybe one of the favourites would be an acquisition and merger strategy? All of these are obvious, simple ideas even if their implementation may not be that easy.

One answer you are unlikely to receive, though, is a serious attempt to maximise added value from the organisation's people. This, for me, is the one and only, truly, organic growth opportunity. Admittedly, all of the improvement strategies cited above require the organisation to mobilise its human resource to deliver its strategy but that is not the same as focusing specifically on the way employees perform and add value.

Many of the significant changes in organisations in the pursuit of step improvements have done precisely the opposite. Take the exponential growth in outsourcing and call centre operations. Here, tasks are oversimplified to ensure that the bulk of the work can be carried out by the technology rather than the people. So when you ring up for an insurance quotation the customer service assistant at the other end has no room for judgement. They just key your details into the database and let the computer do all the work.

I would even go so far as to suggest that normally the *last* resort for most CEOs would be to make a determined effort to really harness the power of their people, despite all their public pronouncements to the contrary. People can be damned awkward. They are just as likely to have their own interests at heart as much, if not more so, than their employer's (and why not?).

Furthermore, although we do not suffer too much these days from the worst excesses of trades unionism (but watch this space), there are many other ways in which people can resist change, particularly change that organisations are forced to instigate due to competitive or regulatory pressures. This all contributes to make managing employee performance a particularly fraught affair – so much so that I am convinced some finance directors would love to run their businesses without any people at all if it were possible.

In general terms, most CEOs look to their market, or potential market, as the source of future growth. Of course they do: any basic understanding of business suggests this is the way to do it. Even public sector bodies today take a view of the market that exists or can be created for their services. But that is always looking outside the organisation. Surely another option is to look at the resources you have inside and to consider how they can best be used. Employees are not just a cost, or a pain in the neck, they are very likely the key to your future existence.

So, even though this may be a relatively new subject, and one that many CEOs have studiously avoided, the diminishing options for future step improvements in organisational performance suggests that now is an ideal time for 'another' book on this subject.

NOT ALL MANAGEMENT BOOKS ARE THE SAME

Walk through the 'management' section of any bookshop and you will see shelves lined with the 'latest' answer to a manager's ills. The vast range of subjects that now come under the generic heading of 'management' is mind-boggling. Yet, have the plethora of management texts that have been produced over the last couple of decades added much to our understanding of how organisations work? Have they unearthed any significant breakthroughs? In particular, are we now better able to harness the full potential of our people to achieve step improvements in organisational effectiveness?

These questions are often debated, especially in academic circles, and from time to time studies will be undertaken to try and provide some answers. However, the very fact that there are so many books still being produced should, in itself, tell us something about *how we learn how to manage*. Maybe the irony of this situation is so subtle that it is lost on many readers of such texts. If there is a vibrant market for so many new texts what does this say about the books that lined the shelves 20 years ago?

ARE THE LATEST MANAGEMENT TEXTS SAYING ANYTHING NEW?

If the management books of 20 years ago had provided us with answers would we still be producing so many texts today? Admittedly, the world has changed beyond all recognition during this period so one might expect that new approaches are now required.

For example, the Taylorist mass production methods, used notably by Ford in the 1920s, which emphasised labour specialisation on repetitive tasks, gradually became anachronistic. But is Taylorism really that far away from the concept of lean production now utilised by most progressive, manufacturing businesses?

Walk into any modern call centre operation today, with their flashing signs showing numbers of calls waiting and calls missed, and you could be forgiven for thinking that the spirit of Taylorism still lives on in some organisations. We could go further and suggest that the dark satanic mill owners of the nineteenth century might also not feel too much out of place in this environment, in spite of the flashy technology.

So do changing times always automatically demand changing approaches to management? Or are there some fundamental lessons of management that each new generation has to relearn and adapt?

DO THE PEOPLE WHO BUY MANAGEMENT BOOKS READ THEM?

If management books are one of the main conduits for new ideas, or even repackaged old ideas, are they actually read by the managers who buy them? Management book publishers generally publish what they think will sell; we could hardly expect them to do otherwise, could we? The books that sell well should also be those readers find useful, hopefully. But that is not always necessarily the case.

Out of the plethora of books published some achieve popularity because they sound so enticing. Who wouldn't want to read Stephen Covey's *7 Habits of Highly Effective People*. This sounds like the modern management version of the old advertisement that offered to help you transform yourself from being a seven-stone weakling. But does the book actually make the reader, themselves, more effective? I could read everything written on John F. Kennedy or Winston Churchill but never be able to emulate them. More importantly, even if they help the individual reader in some way, do such books improve organisational effectiveness?

Busy executives (like you) believe they do not have time to read through the whole of any management text. Consequently, management books are designed to be dipped into or skimmed. They are chopped up into bite-size pieces, like *7 Habits*, with checklists and tools (this book is no different in that particular respect). In other words they are designed to be, first and foremost, digestible. As a result, *the fundamental principles and the bigger picture are so often missed*. This poses a big problem.

Really good management ideas often have a very sound theoretical foundation and are based on a set of solid principles that will stand the test of time. Total quality management (TQM) is a very good example of this. It is a system that can be applied, adapted, developed and refined over an extremely long time period; its potential is possibly even infinite.

However, like most good management systems, it also has some quick and simple practical applications (e.g. produce a histogram showing the causes of customer complaints) which could have an immediately beneficial effect. So the manager dipping into the TQM book is happy that it has been of some use, even though he may never have considered the complete philosophy and principles that underpin TQM.

There is an awful lot more to TQM than immediately meets the eye. To achieve all that TQM has to offer requires a much deeper understanding of the subject than can be garnered from a few quick and dirty tips or tricks. Equally, even the most ardent proponents of TQM, who espouse the philosophy of never-ending, continuous improvement, often do not fully appreciate all the implications and ramifications of their most cherished philosophy.

So, continued success is dependent on someone having a much deeper understanding of the subject. But to gain such a level of understanding obviously requires much more effort from the reader, maybe even a much wider selection of reading. The people who developed the concept of TQM knew about Taylorism. They knew that it had good points as well as bad ones. Most of all, they knew that the earliest versions of Taylorism could never deliver the tough targets that had to be met by organisations in the second half of the twentieth century. Having this wider background knowledge informs your understanding of the subject and influences the way you apply it. If you do not have an understanding of the principles or history of Taylorism then your understanding and implementation of the concept of TQM is incomplete.

How much use you, personally, get out of this book is entirely dependent on your ability to understand it. So to what extent will you understand the text and subtext, the full implications and the practical application of the lessons in this book?

2

Understanding, measurement and learning

- Do you understand? 11
- Kearns' seven levels of understanding 14
- You know you have learned something useful when you get a result 15
- Do the latest management ideas get results? 16
- The perennial subject of measurement 17
- The PDCA cycle is a cycle of performance and learning 20

I will never forget the management meeting where our Head of Quality (we will call him Mike) was presenting the findings of a report that he had just published. This was after many weeks of hard work by him and his team, analysing the causes of some of our most serious quality problems. Within minutes he had lost me. He kept talking about something called x-bar and r-bar charts. (Have you got a clue what they are?)

As he continued talking, I looked at the faces of all the other senior managers around the table. They all looked very intense, as though they were concentrating very hard. Now and again they would indicate how knowledgable they were by nodding their heads when Mike emphasised a particular point. Obviously, it was only me who did not have a clue what Mike was talking about. I thought I would sound stupid if I asked him about these charts.

After about ten minutes though (that was about as much as I could bear) I plucked up the courage to interrupt Mike to say 'Mike, I'm sorry to interrupt but could you just explain, for my benefit, what an x-bar chart is?' Almost instantaneously the other managers all looked up and muttered things like 'Yes, I was just wondering that myself' or 'I'm glad you asked that Paul'.

There is no such thing as a stupid question.

DO YOU UNDERSTAND?

When you ask someone the simple question 'do you understand?' usually you will get a 'yes'. Who wants to admit their ignorance? So, less often, you will get a 'no'; very rarely are people willing to admit they do not understand something, especially in public. How often is the response 'well, I sort of understand' given? It is this last response that has always intrigued me. It suggests that understanding does not work on a binary system, on/off, yes/no. There are gradations of understanding – you can understand a subject a little bit, or in great depth, or anywhere in between. If you want to use employee performance measurement you had better understand the subject in depth.

Having been a trainer for many years my experiences have gradually led me to the conclusion that, whatever you try to 'teach' a group of people on a training programme, the variation in depth of understanding is enormous. Out of a group of, say, 20 participants on a management programme, a few will learn virtually nothing of any practical use. A handful will just absorb the *knowledge* you are trying to impart. Others, more promisingly, understand it enough to put the lessons learned into practice. But only a very small minority attain a depth of understanding which enables them to take the knowledge forward, think through the full implications and use it to make a real difference.

Let us use the study of economics as an example. Do you know what the theory of supply and demand is? As an 'economist' this was one of the first pieces of theory that I had to learn when I was 16 years of age and just starting to study for my A levels.

Actually, I had already learned a great deal about the theory of supply and demand a long time before that, but I was not consciously aware of it. I knew, for example, that the most popular jeans at that time were usually the most expensive. I could never have expressed this knowledge in terms of supply and demand graphs but it was pretty obvious that I would have to pay more for a pair of jeans that all my friends and contemporaries agreed were 'the' jeans to wear. So I had an intuitive understanding of the relationship between supply and demand, albeit without using the correct terminology. Some people would call this common sense – and it is – but having common sense is nowhere near a full understanding of the subject.

My A level economics teacher helped me to express my intuitive grasp of the subject in a much more ordered, systematic way. He explained that, actually, there are *laws* of supply and demand (notice the power of the word laws) which are axiomatic (an academic way of saying pretty obvious or self-evident). Also, to all intents and purposes, they are universally applicable to virtually all markets for goods and services, give or take a few exceptions. So, something that I knew intuitively now moved up to a higher plane of understanding.

During the rest of my A level economics course we returned to the laws of supply and demand again and again. Also, we had to be totally familiar with the application of the practical tools of sketching supply and demand graphs as a means of illustrating different market conditions, quickly and simply.

Perhaps the most important aspect of 'laws', however, is their inherently, *fundamental* nature. If someone were able to prove that the laws of supply and demand did *not* hold, in most circumstances, then the whole theoretical framework of economics would collapse and a new theoretical basis would have to be written.

If you think such a possibility is highly unlikely it is worth noting that, in the field of physics, Einstein published his original thesis on special relativity without a single reference to other, existing academic texts on the subject. He had completely changed the conventional wisdom and theoretical basis of much of the study of physics – and the rest, as they say, is history.

History is more liberally strewn with such fundamental shifts in thinking than you might care to imagine. Remember Dick Fosbury? He was the high jumper who completely changed the standard technique in high jumping to what came to be called the (backward jumping) Fosbury flop. He won an Olympic gold medal to prove his point in Mexico in 1968. Now nearly all high jumpers use this technique.

More recently, in the medical world, researchers had spent years trying to fathom out the causes of cot deaths. Then one research group broke away from conventional advice to tell mothers to lie their babies on their backs. Within three years there was a 50 per cent decrease in cot deaths, in the main attributed to this single piece of simple, yet fundamental, advice

Back to economics for a moment, though. There have been some major changes in economic thinking over the years with big swings from Keynes to Milton Friedman. Fortunately, though, the core fundamentals of supply and demand have not changed.

My full understanding of the laws of supply and demand were only completely developed, however, when I established my own business. The organisations I spoke to found it extremely difficult to express what they needed in simple terms. Their understanding of their own needs was limited. I was constantly having to rethink how the theories of economics applied.

Whatever I read in the economics textbooks, or business case studies, nothing conveyed to me what it was like to really *experience* this. Only when I faced conference audiences and presented my own ideas did I truly realise that there is not only demand but also latent demand that is waiting to be tapped. Also, what organisations said they wanted and what they actually needed could apparently be totally different.

Organisations *needed* solutions to difficult, intractable, structural business problems. What they seemed to *want* was instant, quick-fix, off-the-shelf answers. My understanding of supply and demand had moved not just onto a higher plane, but to an entirely different plane altogether. It was outside the normal boundaries and needed to be much more adaptive.

I am not absolutely sure exactly how many levels of understanding exist. For all I know, this concept may already be the focus of academic research somewhere. What I do know, though, from a practical perspective, is that it is absolutely crucial to realise that the subject of measurement can be approached on different levels. It can be very simple and it can be very profound. It is a relatively new subject and existing levels of understanding on the subject are very limited.

So, as someone who has taken a specialist interest in the subject for ten years (and many more years intuitively before that) I cannot emphasise enough that, if you want to read further, then you had better be prepared to move up to at least one higher level of understanding, if not several. For what it is worth Figure 2.1 gives my list of the seven levels that I recognise.

> **Fig. 2.1** Kearns' seven levels of understanding
>
> Level 1 – Intuitive
> Level 2 – Knowledge
> Level 3 – Principles (basic)
> Level 4 – Application (simple)
> Level 5 – Principles (advanced)
> Level 6 – Adaptive (advanced application)
> Level 7 – Innovative

KEARNS' SEVEN LEVELS OF UNDERSTANDING

Let us look briefly at what the seven levels in Figure 2.1 mean using our understanding of the subject of measurement as an example.

- *Level 1 – Intuitive*

  You intuitively understand that some things need to be measured such as profit and loss.

- *Level 2 – Knowledge*

  You have heard of key performance indicators, critical success factors and even something called the balanced business scorecard.

- *Level 3 – Principles (basic)*

  Perhaps you understand that some of the basic principles of measurement are that you need a scale for comparison and that to measure performance improvements there must be a baseline measure taken first.

- *Level 4 – Application (simple)*

  You understand the principles well enough to start producing tally charts and you can use a performance distribution curve to compare performance (*see* Chapter 7).

- *Level 5 – Principles (advanced)*

  Having tried to measure performance you start to come across some problems. Some performance measures seem to be conflicting and your team start to argue and blame other people for underperformance. You start to realise that added value is a better measure than simple performance.

- *Level 6 – Adaptive*

  You organise a cross-functional meeting to address the issues of performance overlaps between teams and departments. Everyone is shown how to look at the ultimate added value measures.

- *Level 7 – Innovative*

    You now have such an intimate and deep understanding of performance measurement that you start to think about how the principles can be used to develop new ideas. You discuss future added value measures with your team and look for innovative and creative ideas. You ask the team to produce their own performance measures and your role as manager starts to change. A focus on measurable added value is now very closely linked to organisational learning.

If this brief example helps to convince you that there are seven levels to understanding any subject then you might like to try Tool 13 (*see* the appendix) now, but use another subject to focus on. This is particularly interesting when you ask a board of directors how well they understand some of the initiatives they are currently driving!

YOU KNOW YOU HAVE LEARNED SOMETHING USEFUL WHEN YOU GET A RESULT

One really important lesson to learn about measurement is that it is an absolutely key element in learning. It encourages and reinforces personal performance improvement when an individual can see that what they have learned produces results.

For example, you can teach someone to play chess in a relatively short time. You could teach them, in particular, a couple of useful openings. They might even get lucky and win one of their first games, but that is a million miles from producing a grand master.

The best chess players, along with their many other talents, are experts at strategy. They are able to see all the implications of their moves. They can weigh up the pros and cons of possible, alternative strategies very quickly. In essence, their understanding of the game is on a much more profound level. It enables them to play many different opponents and adapt their game accordingly.

What is the point of this analogy? Well, if a chess player were to read numerous books on how to play better chess how would we gauge whether they had learned anything useful? The simplest way would be to measure the level they were able to play at and the number of games they won. That may not be the complete picture but over a period of time it would be an indicator. Certainly we would not consider their reading to have been of much use if they started losing more games than before. A simple, yet crucial, point in performance measurement.

DO THE LATEST MANAGEMENT IDEAS GET RESULTS?

So, following this simple principle, there is, ultimately, only one criterion to be considered when trying to assess the value of any new management idea, that is 'does it work?' Have people learned how to use it properly and does it get real results?

These questions, in turn, can only be answered convincingly by having a believable measure to refer to. No organisation embarks on a course of action to improve its results without asking this question. All investment appraisals have to work on the basis of a cost–benefit equation.

The problem with many new, modern management initiatives (culture change and customer service programmes spring to mind) is that very few of them make a clear connection between the initiative itself, and organisational performance metrics. So no one can actually say whether the initiative worked or not. In spite of this lack of evidence, hope normally triumphs again and again over previous experience, and further initiatives are launched. As usual, though, nobody has bothered to install an effective measurement system first. It is no wonder employees often complain about 'initiative fatigue'.

Where attempts are made at measurement, at best, they just resort to:

- *quasi-measures* which are close to true performance measures but not quite (e.g. productivity per person);
- *pseudo-measures* that look like they are measuring something but in reality are not measuring anything worthwhile (e.g. culture gap analysis); or
- *proxy measures* which are assumed to have a beneficial effect on the business (e.g. employee satisfaction surveys) but do not guarantee that any impact has been achieved.

Classic examples of this sort of approach can be seen in the myriad of 'change programmes' that hard-pressed (or bored?) boards of directors have sanctioned in the vain hope that something will improve. There is no focus on actual results such as a specific level of cost reduction or customer retention. Instead, they employ one of the latest fads, such as a new customer service programme, and measure what they can measure (not what actually matters). In practice this could simply be a measure of how many staff have attended the customer service training programme.

Two eminent academics, Robert H. Schaffer and Harvey J. Thomson, decided to research into this trend and refer to such programmes as 'activity-centred' rather than results-centred. This means that the customer service programme focuses on activity (amount of training) rather than results (perhaps improved profit through greater customer retention). Some of their findings were reported in a 1992 *Harvard Business Review* article ('Successful change programmes begin with results') that eventually became one of the journal's top ten most popular articles. Here is one of their conclusions:

The momentum for activity-centred programmes continues to accelerate even though there is virtually no evidence to justify the investment. Just the opposite: there is plenty of evidence that the rewards from these activities are illusory.

As the title of the article suggests, *the measurable results desired should be the actual focus of the change programme.* Ironically, programmes focused on 'change', *per se*, are unlikely to achieve any change and certainly will not achieve much progress. Schaffer and Thomson appear to have a level 7 understanding of measurement.

THE PERENNIAL SUBJECT OF MEASUREMENT

So, despite everything that has been said so far, will the business world benefit from another book on measurement? As an author who has already had two shots at various facets of this subject, surely there is only so much that can be said on the supposedly boring and limited subject of measurement. Well, apparently not.

A brilliant thinker called Elliott Jacques made some very telling points about both the principles of measurement and the way we learn, simultaneously. He does so by way of reference to the development of an instrument we now all know as the thermometer. He traces the development of this invention back five hundred years to a time when there was not even a universally agreed concept of what heat was. Put another way, they were stuck at the intuitive level of understanding and everyone's intuition was different.

The heat from the sun, from a fire and natural body heat were all perceived as entirely separate phenomena. Needless to say, this 'slight' misunderstanding had to be cleared up before much progress could be made in producing a single device to measure heat. The first building block had to be agreement that heat, regardless of its source, is a single phenomenon. Only then could progress be made in measuring it. Slowly, understanding of the subject developed and grew and it took several hundred years before the first calibrated thermometer was invented.

If it was this difficult to come up with something as straightforward as a thermometer then perhaps we should not be too ambitious or impatient about our ability to measure something as variable as individual performance. But, at least, let us learn that we need a commonly agreed definition of performance.

Accountants thought they had produced their own 'business thermometer' in the form of profit and loss accounts, balance sheets and variance reports. But if the business world had really understood what measurement was all about we would now know exactly which remedies and solutions for organisational ailments actually work and which have proved to be the work of charlatans and alchemists. That is, we would understand what makes successful organisations perform better than their competitors. Yet, conventional accounting practices and measures tell us nothing about the way organisations get the best out of their people.

Meanwhile, as Schaffer and Thomson suggest, the purveyors of the quick-fix, instant panacea (downsizing and business process re-engineering being two of the most misused approaches) seem to be multiplying as we speak. Do a quick search on any Internet-based bookshop, using any of the latest, key buzzwords and check out how many new management texts are being produced almost daily. The latest idea to cross my desk is something called 'reputation management'. How original.

I firmly believe that very few managers actually *read* management books. The skim-readers get hold of the wrong end of the stick or do not follow the complete arguments put forward. In practice this is akin to someone expecting to find a Haynes servicing manual for a Formula One car and being happy enough to strip the engine down having only read the contents page.

Regardless of the reason for it, if management books are not read thoroughly then the original reason for writing them, to teach the reader something, fails. This is probably why management ideas, both old and new, have to be recycled and reiterated several times before the true lessons, that are there to be learned, are fully absorbed. Very, very rarely, though, are there any genuinely new fundamentals of management thinking produced.

We have already referred to TQM, one of the biggest ideas of the twentieth century. Whatever happened to this revolution? Did it die or is it still alive and kicking? Has it assumed another mantle or just been rebadged. Anyone who answers 'we did that ten years ago' or 'we have moved on to the business excellence (European Foundation for Quality Management) model' probably only ever reached level 4. If you cannot see that the EFQM model is just a more detailed, sophisticated version of a system that is at least 70 years old (see the PDCA cycle below) then you are unlikely to understand it in sufficient detail to implement it effectively. You need at least level 5 if not up to level 7.

I was particularly surprised, even shocked, to hear as recently as December 1998 that the 'latest' version of the rather arrogantly titled 'business excellence model' had just been produced. Does this mean that the earlier version did not work very well? Or that the first version was actually wrong? Or am I asking too many embarrassing questions?

If we consider what the EFQM has to say about the importance of people in business excellence, one has to wonder whether they really know what they are talking about. Try visiting www.efqm.org/imodel/modelintro.htm and you will see two headings under their 'fundamental concepts of excellence'. These are:

> *People Development and Involvement*
> *The full potential of an organisation's people is best released through shared values and a culture of trust and empowerment, which encourages the involvement of everyone.*
>
> *Continuous Learning, Innovation & Improvement*
> *Organisational performance is maximised when it is based on the management and sharing of knowledge within a culture of continuous learning, innovation and improvement.*

Do they really understand (at level 7) that there is a connection between performance measurement, learning, empowerment, innovation and continuous improvement? I am not so sure. The EFQM model has leadership on the left and results on the right. The suggestion is that one leads to the other. My view is that the arrow of causation is more likely to point in exactly the opposite direction. Anticipated and planned results drive individual and organisational behaviour and effectiveness.

Like all the best ideas, TQM is basically simple and follows common sense. Quotes such as 'the journey of 1,000 miles starts with one small step' and 'if you don't know your destination you are never going to arrive' are quoted *ad nauseam* because it is so difficult to drum these simple truths into the limited minds of some task-focused, short-termist, operational managers.

The danger of quoting such sayings so regularly is that they become laughable clichés. But this does not mean they have lost any of their essential wisdom. It just means that the same concepts have to be reinvented with different terminology and relaunched if they are ever to be learned.

Take this quote from the learning organisation 'guru' Peter Senge's *The Fifth Discipline Fieldbook* (1994) where his co-authors were amazed at:

> *... how closely our work on learning organisations dovetails with the 'Total Quality' movement ... organisations seriously committed to quality management are uniquely prepared to study the 'learning disciplines'.*

This is a fascinating quote. Obviously it never dawned on the authors that the concept of the 'Fifth Discipline' (systems thinking) was really spawned by intelligent adherence to the philosophy and methodology of TQM over a very long period. It also says a great deal about American intellectual arrogance that they are now suggesting to the TQM experts that they can learn something from Senge. Instead they should be giving full credit to the TQM experts for originating the ideas in the first place! It is not surprising to note that the quality guru,

Deming, received a much warmer welcome for his ideas in Japan in the 1950s than he ever did in the USA.

One of the simplest and best ideas behind TQM is the Plan–Do–Check–Act (PDCA) cycle. This is shown in Figure 2.2 but a more detailed explanation is given in Tool 6 (*see* appendix).

Fig. 2.2 The Plan–Do–Check–Act cycle

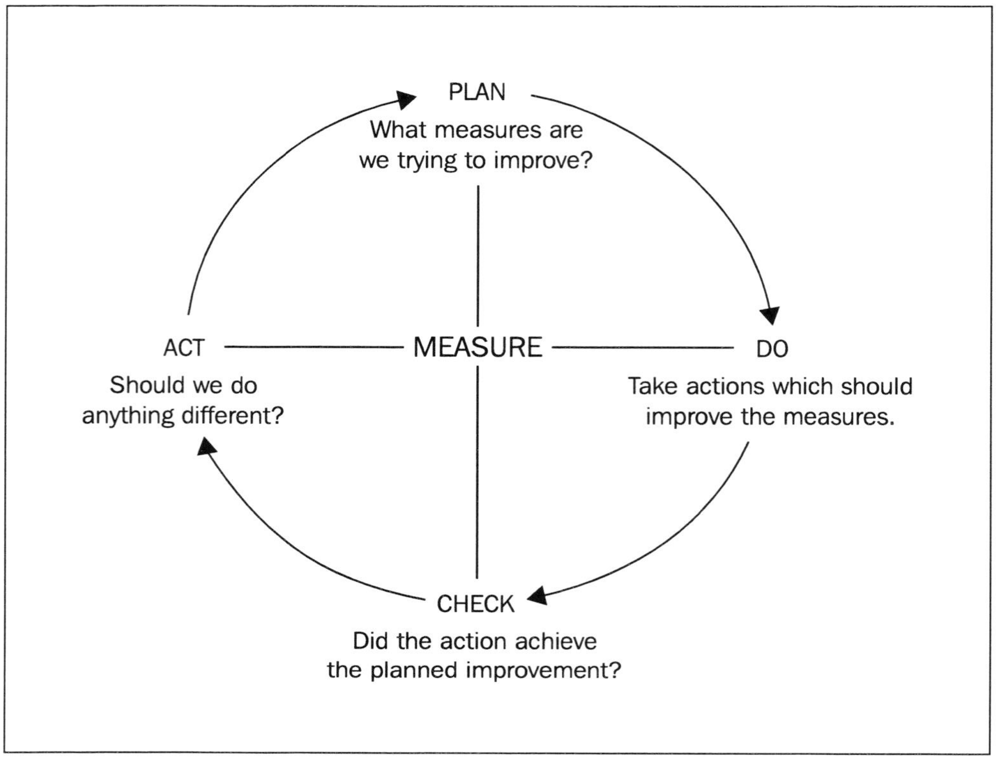

```
                    PLAN
              What measures are
              we trying to improve?

    ACT ─────────── MEASURE ─────────── DO
   Should we do                    Take actions which should
 anything different?                  improve the measures.

                    CHECK
              Did the action achieve
              the planned improvement?
```

THE PDCA CYCLE IS A CYCLE OF PERFORMANCE AND LEARNING

The PDCA cycle can only work effectively when it is based on the use of sound measurements. More importantly, the PDCA cycle is a learning cycle. It tells us whether the improvements that we planned to achieve were actually achieved. This is called 'closing the loop' through honest feedback.

In the early part of 1999 I met a human resources director from a very large, blue-chip business at one of my public seminars. Over lunch he was making a joke about this cycle. The joke was that his business tried the PDCA cycle but in practice resorted to the DDDB system, which apparently stands for Do–Do–Do–Blame! I could see the joke but my laughter was pretty hollow.

'Many a true word is spoken in jest' as they say and, like many jokes, this one masks a very sad indictment of human behaviour. In large organisations, particularly, honest feedback of what works and what does not comes a poor second to personal ambitions, ego and company politics.

It is as important, if not more important, to know when things are *not* working as it is to know when they are working. The old adage, 'we learn from our mistakes' is encapsulated in the PDCA system. So, in effect, the HR director was making a joke about the fact that his company could not use the simplest and most effective organisational improvement and learning system. When viewed from this perspective the joke does not seem half as funny. In fact, it seems positively perverse considering that the joke came from a company striving to be a learning organisation.

Just to emphasise how many seminal ideas are very closely linked take a look at Figure 2.3. This is a simplified version of Kolb's learning cycle.[1] It shows how we learn from the experiences we have. It is almost identical to the PDCA cycle with its planning, experiencing, reviewing and concluding stages. Putting these two ideas together we can see that measurement, learning and improvement are just three facets of the same process. They all fit together perfectly.

Fig. 2.3 A version of Kolb's learning cycle

- Plan – based on experience
- Having an experience
- Reviewing the experience
- Concluding from the experience

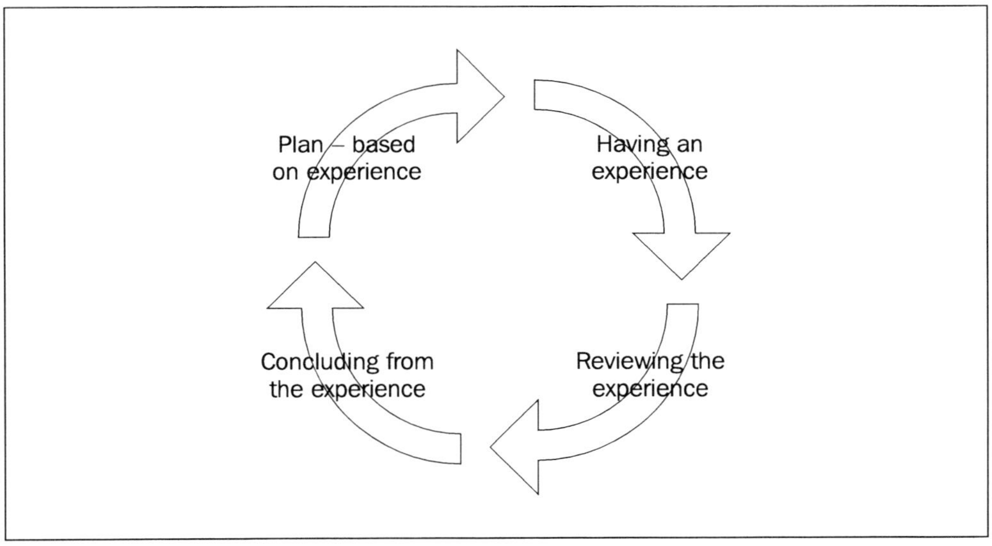

Note

1. Kolb (1984) refers to four stages of concrete experience, reflective observation, abstract conceptualisation and active experimentation. I much prefer this simpler terminology.

3

We measure everything but we're not very good at it

- We measure everything but we're not very good at it 25
- The principles of employee performance measurement 26
- A definition of employee performance measurement 28
- Data, performance information and other terminology 29

WE MEASURE EVERYTHING BUT WE'RE NOT VERY GOOD AT IT

It is quite funny pointing out to people who say 'you can't measure everything' that in fact they do measure almost everything. Who has not said, with incredulity, '*how* much?' on an occasion when they believe an item to be overpriced, whether it is the price of a round of drinks, a spare part for their car or a theatre ticket for a new musical? They do not have an immediate list of comparable prices but something elicits a startled reaction. They have checked the price against their own mental scale and it triggered an 'expensive!' response.

Even if we are not talking about exact prices or precise quantities we all still form a view on how good or bad something is. Descriptions of a pint of beer, regardless of its price, can range anywhere from something the cat might have passed to pure nectar. These are all measures and usually form part of a continuous scale of assessment that ranges from very low to very high.

The measures we use are, very often, highly subjective. They may not be part of a *coherent* measurement system but, nevertheless, they can be called measures for that is what they are and, more importantly, we make decisions based on such measures.

There are two very important points to make here. First, we can improve our methods of measurement enormously. The drinker could ask five friends what they thought of the beer from a certain pub. Second, our personal measurement systems significantly influence our behaviour. So, if the majority of the drinkers' friends give the beer a low rating (each on their own subjective scale) then it is unlikely that the drinker will visit that particular pub.

No one will worry too much if our own measurement systems are not as precise as they could be. However, in an organisational setting, if we do not address the issue of improving measurement systems then we should expect to witness some ridiculous behaviour.

A communications director in a large public sector organisation came to the startling conclusion that there were 'too many' meetings taking place and the 'quality' of the meetings was questionable. This was a purely subjective assessment of the situation as no metrics were collected to prove, or disprove, his thesis. The 'solution' was a 'making meetings better' training pack.

Needless to say, subsequent efforts to resolve this *unmeasured* problem floundered very quickly. No measurement meant no priority. Furthermore, no individual performance measurement meant that no one was to be held accountable and, therefore, everyone thought it was somebody else's problem.

The point here is that although no overt, explicit, objective measurement took place, there was still a genuine belief that a problem existed. Not only that, but a problem of sufficient size to warrant a solution – in this case a training programme. In effect, a subjective 'measurement' had resulted in action.

However, if a higher quality measurement had been used perhaps the problem would have been better understood (*certain* people did not run meetings well). The solution would then have been designed better (focus on a target group), and the matter resolved more quickly, effectively and efficiently (training only for a particular group, who had agreed they needed training, to improve their performance).

Bad measurement takes place all the time but it happens so imperceptibly, unconsciously and yet insidiously that we do not know that it is happening and what damage it is causing. This is particularly true of people measurement. How many times are casual remarks made about someone's performance without being substantiated by any clearly objective measurement? 'She doesn't treat her staff very well', 'he's a terrible communicator', 'he's always late', etc. Often, when such statements are challenged, the accuser is unable to substantiate their original assessment from a better measurement standpoint. Or, their assessment of the individual concerned was actually based on only one quick, isolated observation, which cannot be regarded as a true representation of their performance.

THE PRINCIPLES OF EMPLOYEE PERFORMANCE MEASUREMENT

Whatever Tom Peters says about what makes an excellent organisation the single, most common distinguishing factor, for me, is that the really good organisations have a solid set of clear principles to work to and they tend to stick to those principles. The UK 24-hour telephone bank First Direct (part of the HSBC group) has a superb reputation for customer service. In a customer communication announcing its tenth birthday as a business in 1999 stated under the heading 'How we like to do business ...':

> ... *it's time to clarify the principles on which First Direct was founded. Principles that we continue to work with today ... We aim to give every customer real value, clarity, control, choice and fairness when it comes to any financial need. Anything less at any time is never an option. It's one thing to say it, another to achieve it.*

Obviously the cynics would regard this as mere marketing rhetoric but customers of First Direct (including me) know different. Consider my own anecdotal evidence. When applying for a First Direct mortgage (which incidentally happened to be the best deal around at the time) I returned the wrong form, which could have delayed my house move. When I contacted First Direct to point this out I apologised for the error. The First Direct customer service assistant would have none of it. She immediately accepted blame on behalf of the bank. Having pointed out that it was actually *I* who had returned the wrong form, she still came back at me saying it was their fault.

After a couple more minutes of both trying to accept the blame, she finally convinced me that, regardless of the fact that I had sent them the wrong form, it was their responsibility to check the incoming forms and notify the customer immediately of any problems. When she put it that way I had to agree. But surely the point of this story is that even when they make mistakes they seem to win more customer loyalty. They stick to their principles because it makes good business sense.

So what exactly are principles? The *Oxford Dictionary* definition says a principle is 'a fundamental truth or law, a personal code of conduct'. If principles are fundamental laws then they do not normally change much, if at all, over a very long period of time. Also, as something that guides personal conduct (let us call this behaviour) we can immediately see that sound principles lead to sound behaviour.

Honesty is the best policy. This is a principle which most of the human race would subscribe to and yet not one of us adheres to this principle 100 per cent. This does not mean that we stop trying to stick as close to this principle as we can. It is something to constantly aim for because we all know it makes sense. This is a lesson that we would do well to take to heart when we try to measure performance.

Having the right principles is therefore extremely important. So, regardless of what currently happens in employee performance measurement in your organisation, before we move any further forward it is a good idea to be absolutely clear what principles we should follow (*see* Figure 3.1).

Fig. 3.1 The guiding principles of employee performance measurement

- Measures should be easily expressed and simple to understand.
- They should be meaningful in size and importance.
- They should be agreed, accepted and motivating.
- You can't manage what you don't measure.
- But don't just measure what you can.
- What gets measured gets done.
- A baseline and target performance measure should always be established.

Failure to follow any one of the principles listed in Figure 3.1 will render the employee performance measurement and management system (or EPMMS, pronounced ee-pems) much less effective than it could be. If several of the principles are ignored then it is highly likely that the EPMMS will fail.

Principles are just the starting point, however. The next step is to be absolutely clear as to what constitutes a reasonable, meaningful, performance measurement. So, at the risk of being pedantic, we had better define, as precisely as this subject allows, what exactly we mean by performance measurement.

A DEFINITION OF EMPLOYEE PERFORMANCE MEASUREMENT

We can define an employee performance measurement as:

A conscious, objective assessment of the extent to which an individual is fulfilling or exceeding the requirements of their role, both in absolute and comparative terms. Moreover, performance measures are primarily intended to foster continuous improvement.

Some of the key words here are:

- *conscious* – if you ask someone to produce an employee performance measure they should be absolutely clear what is required and make a conscious effort to produce something meaningful.
- *objective* – objectivity is crucial: where is the evidence to support the assessment?
- *absolute* – the minimum we expect from a performance measure is whether the employee is working at an acceptable level. This implies we have a baseline to work from.
- *comparative* – we would also like to know how they are performing in comparison to their own work colleagues or similar employees elsewhere.
- *continuous improvement* – the main reason for having performance measures is to generate continuous individual and organisational improvement. Continuity is a key concept.

If this is a workable definition then let us consider how closely some conventional performance measures match this definition. You might think that spending time discussing terminology is mere semantics. Perhaps the discussion above, about perceptions of what is and what is not measurement, will serve as a reminder that accurate terminology can be very important. Consequently we need to quickly revisit some of the most used and abused words in performance measurement.

You might also like to try Tool 10 (*see* appendix) to look at some examples of good employee performance measures.

DATA, PERFORMANCE INFORMATION AND OTHER TERMINOLOGY

First on the list is the old chestnut, data versus *information*. We want performance information, not just piles of meaningless data. Data only becomes information when it is used for decision making. A trainer told me that one employee had failed to achieve an acceptable standard in a particular piece of training despite several attempts over several years. This data was presented to various managers but nothing was done about it. Presenting this as information with impact (e.g. this employee is costing us £50,000 per annum in salary and rework) might get a decision.

Ideally, as we have already highlighted, we want performance information to be *objective* rather than subjective. Performance assessments will always involve personal views and opinions but, wherever possible, these should be backed up with hard evidence.

Qualitative information is inherently based on value judgements and is often confused with quality measures (e.g. error rates), an entirely different thing. It can be useful in performance measurement but should be allied to harder, objective measures. A beer company observes its salespeople, after training, in face-to-face situations with customers. From this, the trained observer feeds back to the salesperson comments about their behaviour. These are qualitative assessments, but only when sales figures are used, in conjunction with these observations, will they be truly meaningful.

The very term *measure*, itself, can cause all sorts of problems. A measurement is only a true measure when it is related to a scale or yardstick. In performance terms the yardstick can be minimum standards, targets or comparative performance, internally or externally.

Finally, performance measures will always be measures of *outputs*. Your organisation only exists because of its outputs. A local authority outputs street lighting, refuse collection and other services. A hospital outputs healthy patients (hopefully). A beer company outputs beer. There may be many more 'outputs', though, that lead to these final outputs: the clerk who takes a call about a missed refuse collection, the hospital records clerk who keeps accurate patient information, the drayman who delivers the beer to the outlet. These can all be regarded as outputs, but beware any measure that only looks at inputs and know the difference.

Now is a good time to consider what, if any, principles are being used to underpin performance in your organisation.

4

Revisiting performance measurement

- Why performance measurement needs to change   33
- How performance measurement needs to change   36
- The balanced business scorecard in practice   38

Many experienced line and operational managers may think that the latest focus on performance measurement is unlikely to lead to anything particularly new or useful. This does not include you, of course – you are reading this book. What about your colleagues, though? What are they reading at the moment?

After all, they have been working towards performance targets every day of their working lives. The better ones also do their best to achieve targets *through* their people. They may have their own particular methods, a combination of carrot and stick maybe, but ultimately they see that they can only achieve their targets by ensuring each member of their team makes a contribution.

Regardless of how good any particular manager is at managing performance, though, there are many reasons why the subject is now in need of a fundamental review.

WHY PERFORMANCE MEASUREMENT NEEDS TO CHANGE

Managers cannot manage in a vacuum

It is quite natural for any manager to want to be in control of his or her own destiny, as much as possible. They are also prepared to accept responsibility and accountability for their own particular part of the operation. Yet no individual, team or department is an island. The structure and processes that the organisation is built on automatically link each area of the overall operation (*see* Chapter 14). So 'vacuum-packed' measures are not as appropriate as they perhaps once were. Performance measurement must cross over the functional silos and organisational hierarchies.

Achievement of this month's targets does not guarantee the continued achievement of future targets

A manufacturing company I used to work for, in the automotive components sector, was asked by one of its major customers to reduce its prices by 5 per cent. Around the boardroom table we discussed how we could achieve this and, one way or another, we believed we could find efficiencies that would enable us to reduce prices by 5 per cent.

The following year the same scenario arose: a further 5 per cent reduction. We scratched our heads a bit harder and came up with some ideas for reducing prices through further efficiencies. Again, the following year – you guessed it – exactly the same situation arose with exactly the same response. It does not take a genius to realise that, at some stage in this process, the management team were soon going to run out of ideas to meet the enforced price reductions.

That said, I do not remember anyone on the board (including me) saying that if this was going to happen *ad infinitum* then we were looking at reducing our cost base significantly, to such an extent that we would have to envisage running the operation, in five years' time, 25 per cent more efficiently than we currently could. If we had considered our situation from this perspective for one moment then maybe we would all have taken a fresh look at the longer term and stopped being so reactive.

Being reactive in performance measurement misses the whole point. If we were to achieve the significant level of cost savings needed to stay in business, we had to fundamentally rethink our ways of operating (*see* Chapter 13). We could not expect line managers to deliver the goods every time without involving them in thinking through longer-term solutions. Also, if we needed innovative ideas to rise to the challenge, at some stage we would have to involve employees at all levels. They would always know more about detailed operational opportunities than any manager could.

Otherwise, all we were really doing was increasing pressure and stress levels without addressing the longer-term, underlying business issues. We made no attempt to think through how we needed to fundamentally change our approach to managing our people.

Making a connection between performance and learning

The most disappointing aspect of traditional performance measurement systems is that they completely miss the opportunities for encouraging learning. To achieve improved performance people have to learn how to work more efficiently or effectively. Learning is the key. Some of the lessons to be learned may be very simple and quick, such as how to draw a tally chart to highlight causes of errors. Other important lessons may take much longer, such as cause and effect analysis. However, *those who are trying to learn, only truly learn when they start to experience an improvement* (i.e. error rates reduce).

So performance improvement and learning are almost synonymous. Logically, therefore, if performance measurement is poorly focused this will result in inferior learning. The best example of this I have seen was when I was working with a large public sector organisation on performance appraisal. As part of the programme I was running we held some dummy appraisal discussions between the managers on the programme. Listening in on one of these discussions, I heard the appraiser say 'so do you think you can achieve a 5 per cent improvement in this next year' to which the appraisee replied 'yes'. Then they quickly moved on to the next item.

I stopped the discussion to ask whether this was really a stretch objective because the appraisee did not sound stretched. More importantly, if they were not being stretched to what extent would the performance target make them think and learn? Moreover, what would they learn next year that would help them achieve even tougher targets the following year?

Continuous and self-generating performance improvement

Because the traditional approach to performance measurement has been to *impose* measures it has not encouraged continuity. Once one target was reached there would be a sigh of relief until the next target was imposed.

However, implicit in much of what has been said so far is the need to ensure continuous improvement. Setting monthly, yearly or budgetary targets will always concentrate minds on the task in hand. Take away the targets and the generation of improvement ideas can come to a halt.

Although most organisations have now had to accept that the pressure to continuously improve is relentless, it does not necessarily mean that their employees have any more enthusiasm for what can appear to be a future of pressure and stress. Later, we will consider what effect a performance-based reward system can have on individual and team performance. However, *every opportunity should be taken to motivate people rather than enforce performance improvements.*

Although this can be difficult, *one of the simplest and easiest ways is to involve all employees in the setting of performance measures*. Although someone needs to ensure they are the right measures, it is surprising how willing some employees are to set their own improvement measures. In fact, they are often much more ambitious than their boss would ever have dreamt.

Changes in management style – empowering and involving employees

The previous item may have really frightened you. The idea of handing a key management tool, performance measurement, over to your staff sounds like one of the prime roles of a manager has just been delegated. So what does it leave for managers to do?

Well this is exactly where performance measurement is heading. When senior managers run out of ideas on efficiency improvements line managers have to start thinking. Line managers cannot know every detail of the operation, though, so when they have achieved some efficiencies their last resort is to start asking their team to look for opportunities. This inevitably means that employees become much more directly involved. In turn, in order to achieve improvements at a micro level, there is a logical move towards empowering employees to make more decisions for themselves rather than waiting to be told what to do. Empowerment is a much more efficient, if riskier, approach to management.

Empowerment frightens managers for two main reasons. It certainly undermines their own position, but it can also be dangerous for the organisation because empowering employees, without ensuring they are capable and trained to be empowered, can mean selecting the wrong measures and lead to the wrong activity.

HOW PERFORMANCE MEASUREMENT NEEDS TO CHANGE

Holistic and integrated performance measurement

Another broad reason for revisiting performance measurement is that we have learned from experience that setting individual, disjointed measures completely ignores the fact that any operating unit in any organisation is part of a holistic entity. It cannot be broken up into completely separate chunks for performance measurement purposes.

How well your car is serviced is not just down to the mechanic. The complete service is dependent on everyone in the chain, including the booking clerk, the parts department and even the valeter. You will only be totally satisfied if all of these people perform.

Let us look at one operational unit, say a single ward in a hospital. Although some simple measures could be set for its efficiency, its overall performance has to be viewed on a broader front. This is dependent on the range of consultants and other medical staff who have patients on the ward, the portering staff, cleaners, suppliers of services (both internal and external) as well as all the administrative and support services that come into contact with that ward. So, if one key performance measure was patient satisfaction, only a holistic approach to this will ensure it is maximised.

Obviously, in practice, this would mean all of those involved with this ward would have to submit to the same overall performance measures, as well as their own specific measures (e.g. external suppliers have to deliver within 24 hours). Sharing performance measures makes sense and focuses everyone on the ultimate objectives, so it is worthwhile aiming to apply holistic measures. This also leads to the idea of balancing performance measures.

Balancing performance measures

Over the years management methods have become increasingly sophisticated and refined. Economies of scale, improved technology and straightforward efficiency improvements have led many organisations onto an entirely different plane in performance terms. One only has to look at the ease with which bills can be paid or goods ordered over the phone to realise this.

As performance pressures increase, one problem that arises is that the measures can start to conflict with each other. The marketing team are focused on increasing market share but the product developers are trying to reduce their costs. Also, focusing on a few narrow measures such as costs may drive down costs but have a disproportionate effect on quality.

For a variety of reasons, therefore, it became apparent that narrow financial and operational measures were unable to deliver the greater levels of performance needed to stay competitive in a tough marketplace. The successful organisations would be those that were able to harness every aspect of their organisation and focus it on improvement, in other words those that got every part of the equation right, the right balance between competing objectives and effective measures.

It was this sort of realisation that has led to ideas such as the balanced business scorecard (BBS) approach to performance measurement. While there is a proprietary version of this model, many organisations have latched onto the concept at its simplest level (level 4) and now produce management information across a whole spectrum of measures, supposedly in a balanced way.

Before I say anything else about the BBS, though, the word 'scorecard' should be emphasised. Although this is meant to be a management tool it is, as its name declares loudly and clearly, first and foremost about scores or measurement. It stands or falls, therefore, by the quality or meaningfulness of the measures chosen. Without measures it is nothing.

That said, my view is that the BBS is an intelligent response to a very complex problem. How can you put together a coherent measurement framework that pulls together and balances what can often appear to be conflicting forces?

You may never have seen it this way but there is a multitude of competing and conflicting pressures on organisations. Even the basic business proposition of 'look after your customers and your customers will look after you' is founded on a relationship that is inherently one of conflict. Most entrepreneurs really want to create a monopoly position so that they can achieve the greater returns that this allows. On the other hand, customers want plenty of competition for the purposes of choice and lower prices. Businesses and customers are pulling in different directions.

Despite the rhetoric of excellent customer service and the avowed aim of 'delighting the customer', company behaviour often clearly demonstrates a lack of genuine commitment to putting the customer first. On the other side of the equation, most customers are only as loyal as your prices, quality and level of service deserve. The growing use of e-commerce will make this fact of life even more apparent than it ever was before.

What brings these two conflicting forces together is some sort of balance. Good companies try to give the best customer service they can at the prices they are charging. Competition tends to make them do this. The ones that aim to keep satisfying their customers, more than their competitors, try to make sure every aspect of their operation works in harmony towards this end. Using the BBS is meant to be one way of achieving this.

In theory, and in principle, the BBS is a good idea but how well does it work in practice?

THE BALANCED BUSINESS SCORECARD IN PRACTICE

Figure 4.1 was taken from a conference presentation by a manager from NatWest Bank, a large retail bank that was using a putative balanced business scorecard approach in 1993. Like many large organisations looking for the latest panacea, it was pretty obvious that the level of understanding on the concept was probably about level 2.

Fig. 4.1 A balanced scorecard?

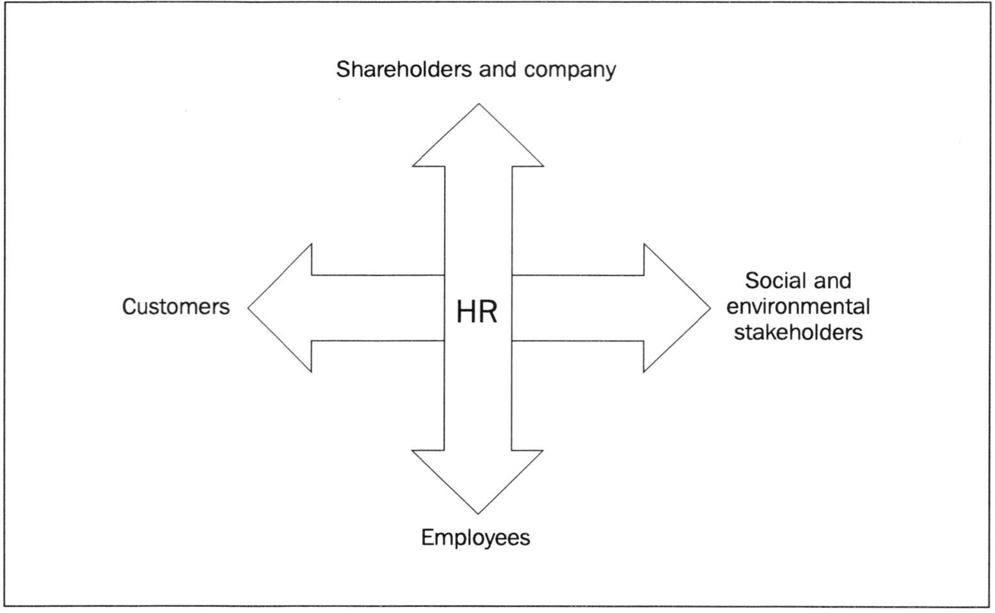

[Diagram showing four arrows radiating from "HR" at the center pointing to: Shareholders and company (up), Customers (left), Social and environmental stakeholders (right), Employees (down)]

The proprietary BBS refers to four main areas or 'perspectives' on setting objectives and measures. The generic perspectives are financial, customer, internal processes and learning and growth. The inventors of the proprietary product, Robert S. Kaplan and David P. Norton, had come to the conclusion that unless a business managed to balance all of these elements it was less likely to succeed in meeting its strategic objectives.

You will notice from Figure 4.1 that somewhere along the way the basic tenets of the theory and conceptual framework by Kaplan and Norton have been lost. There is no reference to the word processes, for example. Also, where did social and environmental stakeholders come from? Here we see a brilliant example of the enormous difference between the textbook and the practice. The original concept, as in so many management ideas, has already been fundamentally altered.

As always, though, what gets measured gets done (one of the principles of measurement). In this case, NatWest's scorecard had pushed them towards adopting a more environmentally friendly car fleet. On a visit to a NatWest office in London at the time, I happened to read an internal employee magazine story referring to the bank's policy of converting its car fleet to diesel engines. This project was just nearing completion only two weeks after the latest, most authoritative study on exhaust emissions had come down in favour of petrol over diesel engines. Their environmental stakeholders would not have been impressed.

The main criticism I would level at the original BBS concept is that, while the framework is reasonably sound, the key perspective for me is learning and growth and yet this is the one where meaningful measures have yet to be developed. As a specialist in HR measurement I have to say that most efforts I have witnessed to address the people measures perspective have been rather meaningless.

This is precisely the perspective that this book is addressing, the people measures. However, before we look in any more detail at the theory and concepts of employee performance measurement, we need to consider some of the immediate practicalities.

Part 2

How to do it – the tricks of the trade

- 5 But I don't want to be measured   43
- 6 Management information systems and people performance   53
- 7 The performance measurement proposition   63
- 8 Performance and added value are not the same   81
- 9 Motivation and performance – what's the connection?   89
- 10 Rewarding performance   95
- 11 Performance appraisal and assessment   103
- 12 Key people – critical performance   113

5

But I don't want to be measured

- The psychological contract 45
- Resistance to measurement 46
- The positive side of measurement 47

THE PSYCHOLOGICAL CONTRACT

Do you *deserve* a better performance from your employees? If you have not spent much time thinking about this subject stop now and consider the perspective of one of your staff. Why should they want to perform better? If your answer is 'well, if they want to stay in a job ...' go to the back of the class.

What contract do you have with your employees? I do not mean what is in writing. How much interest have you shown in them and how much effort do you expect in return? Are they working in your organisation, despite the pay being low, because they have never had to work too hard? Conversely, do they want to work there because the pay is good but feel no special sense of loyalty? Or are they just not particularly amenable to demands for performance improvement?

The relationship between employer and employee is quite complex. Employers place demands on their workforce but realise there will always be a quid pro quo. Likewise, for most employees, there is a balance to be struck between the need to earn a crust and wanting something more out of their work. You, yourself, may be a considerate people manager but there are always conflicting demands on your time and there is always the work that has to be completed by the end of the day.

Over a long period of time an unwritten, psychological contract develops that is never made entirely explicit. Traditionally, the public sector, for example, has not offered the greatest rewards, but neither was it regarded as pressurised a workplace as most commercial working environments. Now, the pressures to deliver and be accountable are increasing (the concept of 'best value' is the latest government wheeze to exhort public sector bodies to do so) but has the 'psychological contract' been correctly 'rewritten' or do they still expect the old contract to continue?

In some commercial concerns there is a culture of 'hours', the sort of culture that suggests the best performing employees are those who spend the highest number of hours at work. This tends to encourage people to make sure their car is the first in the car park in the morning and the last one there in the evening. As a performance measurement specialist I have to say my experience shows that 'hours worked' is a very poor and inconsistent indicator of actual performance. Hours at work are not necessarily even an indicator of individual effort.

Any organisation wanting to be a 'high performance' organisation will probably have a large number of hard working employees, but if they ever confuse input with performance output they will be reinforcing the wrong types of behaviour.

Another angle on the psychological contract is the unwritten set of rules for management style. Do managers still prepare budgets with plenty of 'fat' in them, in the expectation of having to make cuts in the final round of negotiations? Do they only agree objectives that they know they can meet or are they really prepared to stretch themselves and their staff? Or is pure politics and image the order of the day? Do you survive in this organisation on the cut of your suit and the gloss of your presentations?

When you introduce a really effective EPMMS it will start to cut across these unwritten 'contracts'. It will shake up existing attitudes and perceptions and scrape off the veneer of managerial hype. Everyone in the organisation will be confronted with reality in a way they may never have been before. So be prepared for some resistance and consider how you are changing the psychological contract. We will return to this issue in Chapter 15 but for now we have to think of the immediate practicalities.

RESISTANCE TO MEASUREMENT

You might think that the biggest obstacle to good performance measurement is the simple fact that measurement itself can be difficult. This *is* a big obstacle but not as big as the even more obvious obstacle of human resistance.

Mention the subject of 'measuring people' to most managers and you immediately observe a resigned expression followed swiftly by a tired litany of excuses as to why the two words 'people' and 'measurement' do not go very well together in the same sentence.

As a specialist in this subject, I think I must have heard every possible excuse for not wanting to use people performance measures. One of the most ludicrous objections has to be that apparently 'you cannot measure the things that really matter'. Their own logic (*sic*) is their undoing. How can you know what matters if you have not measured it?

By 'the things that matter' I guess they normally mean such esoteric subjects as morale and motivation or communication. Interestingly, I have yet to meet an organisation that does not believe that it has a communication problem. They have never truly measured it though – which probably explains, simultaneously, why the problem exists in the first place and why they have never managed to solve it!

At the root of resistance to individual measurement is the unfortunate fact of life that measurement of individuals means an increase in their accountability. When I know how well or badly someone is performing I can start to hold them accountable. This is not a problem for good performers who will happily encourage, never mind accept, measurement because it is one way of providing the recognition they are usually seeking.

Another reason for much resistance is the very activity of measuring, itself, which can seem either daunting, highly bureaucratic or just simply boring, especially the sort of measuring normally associated with people. Timesheets, absence forms and even employee assessments all seem like an enormous chore. The fact of the matter is, they are.

Once measurement is perceived as a chore it will rarely be carried out properly, if at all. Employee performance measurement has to become an integrated part of the way the organisation operates. It is for this reason that, wherever possible, existing measurement systems should be utilised as much as possible. Data capture and collation can be a very time-consuming business so the less extra work the better.

The real trick is to *see existing measures from a people performance angle and personalise them wherever you can*. For example, a brewery may measure tonnage delivered per person, which the logistics and accounts departments will be keen to monitor. But this tells us nothing about the individual range of performances achieved by the delivery drivers. Surely it is of interest to everyone, including the delivery drivers, to know what the best and worst performers can achieve.

THE POSITIVE SIDE OF MEASUREMENT

To overcome resistance to performance measurement we must endeavour to generate interest in the subject. Not only that, measurement should be perceived as something positive and constructive and not a means for blaming or putting pressure on employees. This can be quite a difficult trick to pull off. So, in order to do this, there are four very important factors in promoting employee performance measurement to a wary audience.

Excitement

We should try to produce performance measures that are exciting. Part of the excitement comes from taking a risk, preferably a calculated risk. When we set out to improve performance there are no guarantees that it is actually going to happen. As Charles Handy so perceptively remarked in *Understanding Organisations* (1992) there is an:

> *... inherent ability of the human being to override many of the influences on his (her) behaviour.*

A great deal of effort may be expended in exhorting employees to perform better but they will only improve if they want to or are forced to. I think the former option is definitely the one I favour.

So how do you use measurement to excite people? Well, how about looking at a terrible example first. A 'new' university was trying to adopt all sorts of the latest management techniques to bring itself up to speed with some of the more established and thrusting academic institutions. Part of this drive included the use of the now ubiquitous 'mission statement'. Each school in the university had its own mission statement and the one devised by the school of engineering was that they wanted to become the seventh best engineering school in the country! How energising and motivating. No doubt they were looking for the seventh best engineering academics as well!

Would joining the seventh best department motivate you? Admittedly, not every engineering department can be number one but blind adherence to the use of mission statements completely misses the point. Maybe a better mission would have been to be number one in added value engineering higher education. This could be measured by looking at the number of firsts awarded (outputted) compared to the input level of the students (average A level scores). They could be number one in added value without having the highest number of firsts.

Mission statements are meant to be stretching. Employees are intended to buy into what they aim to achieve. They are supposed to galvanise organisational effort and improve *esprit de corps*. A mission statement is a performance objective and this sort of mission statement gives the whole concept a bad name.

So how do you excite employees in organisations that are never likely to be number one? One simple idea can be taken from the world of athletics, the personal best. Many athletes know in their heart of hearts that they are never going to win Olympic gold but it does not stop them trying. All they can do is aim to keep improving on their personal best and just hope that this moves them nearer and nearer to that ultimate goal. The challenge is as motivating and almost as rewarding as the goal itself.

It is a fact of life that some people are more talented, productive and creative than others. This does not mean that the 'poorest performers' are not doing their best. Neither does it mean that organisations should only try to attract and retain the best – this would just lead to a whole range of different problems, such as trying desperately to satisfy everyone's career aspirations.

What it does mean, though, is that the best organisations get the best out of the people they have. The employees themselves need to know what their own current 'best' is and believe that they can improve on it. This is what performance measurement is all about.

When setting performance objectives *the very act of setting the objective should excite the employee* and not switch them off. This is not idealistic claptrap. Give any employee ten objectives and then review which ones showed the most progress. I will guarantee that they will first be the objectives that the employee saw as mandatory and secondly those that excited the employee. Do not expect much progress on those objectives to which you, or the employee, were indifferent.

To be exciting, performance measures should be significant. This is not necessarily the same as saying they should be aiming to make a big improvement in absolute terms. Runners who specialise in the 100 metre dash would do anything to shave a hundredth of a second off their time and will be very pleased if they can achieve this, even if they are still one second short of the best.

So what would a significant performance objective be for a call centre operative? The number of calls they might handle may not excite them but maybe a 1 per cent increase in conversion rates would. What might be even more exciting is converting this to a £ sign. If 1 per cent equals £10,000 this might be exciting whereas if it equals 4p it will not.

All of this, of course, should also be clearly seen as part of the bigger picture. The call centre company may have a drive to improve conversion rates across the board by 1 per cent, which equates to £500,000 on the bottom line. Every employee who contributes their own 1 per cent to this should be excited by the prospect of their own contribution to this much bigger sum.

Motivation

Excitement is one thing, motivation is another. Yes, the two should be very closely linked but, as a trainer, I have seen too many trainees leave a course very excited only to have their motivation squashed when they return to work. Also, you might get very excited about working for a company that wants to be number one but you will only be motivated to do things which you believe are possible.

Another motivational angle on this is the whole idea of setting stretch objectives. There is not much satisfaction in achieving an objective that was easy. Performance measures should make employees think and learn new ways of doing things. By achieving the objective they can be confident that they have learned something in the process. This is the win–win of performance measurement.

A pat on the back always helps as well. I had a holiday job as a student, many years ago, in a large hotel that was part of a well-known national chain. A major part of the job seemed very unrewarding. It just involved polishing the floor of the main corridor between reception and the bedrooms, every morning, using an industrial polisher. It took about five minutes to learn how to do this job and another five to become totally bored with it, except that one day a guest passed by while I was working on the floor and remarked how beautifully shiny it was. Almost instantaneously I took a greater pride in my work from this verbal pat on the back. I even pushed the polisher into all the corners and then started using a cloth by hand for the areas I could not reach. The compliments started to increase and became more regular and this boring job somehow did not seem as completely boring as it used to be.

Action

With excitement and motivation we can hope to get action and results. What do I mean by this? We will see throughout this book that individual performance, *per se*, is only part of the picture. The performance of each one of us is often dependent on the performance of others. Only if we all act in concert will the organisation obtain the benefit.

One of the classic problems with performance improvement initiatives is the perception of who can and cannot have an impact on organisational performance. Some sections of the organisation are deemed to be excluded from the whole process (e.g. the accounts department) or, alternatively, there is a belief that performance is only attributable to one function (e.g. sales or production). This could simply be so because no one has made the right connections. Alternatively, strong characters at director level, playing power politics, want it to appear that way. In more traditional environments it could also be that the traditional power base lies within a certain clique (perhaps the buyers in retail) or the organisation is afraid to slaughter a few sacred cows (e.g. they do not want to offend their technical experts) in the cause of performance management.

The best example I have seen of this happening is in the Lloyds insurance market in London. The gods of some broking houses are the insurance brokers themselves. Despite the débâcle at Lloyds in the 1980s and 1990s these people still try to obtain business through traditional channels of contacts, networks and a liberal sprinkling of heavy lunches. Unfortunately for them, the tide is turning and those businesses that want to remain successful in this market are beginning to get their houses in order.

When organisations start to come under unprecedented pressure from external forces, rather than deciding to fundamentally reinvent themselves, they think the easiest option is just to focus on improved efficiency. Usually this means, in practice, that the cost of support functions comes under the greatest scrutiny because they are perceived to be non-added value. So they have to become super-efficient and new technology is introduced to handle most of the simplest, repetitive tasks.

In one particular case there was a crystal clear performance target set for the business. It had a cost/income ratio of over 100 per cent (it was losing money) and it had aimed to reduce this, at least, to 95 per cent. However, it soon became apparent that much of the support staffs' time was expended putting right errors or omissions that should have been sorted out at the broking stage of the insurance process. But most of their brokers, apparently, were only interested in generating business and could not be bothered to cross all the t's and dot all the i's. So support staff efficiency was undermined by the brokers' underperformance – not a brilliant business situation to be in.

When the time came to improve the performance of back office staff by reducing the time it took to produce a policy document, things could not improve much as most of the delays were due to their having to chase brokers for vital pieces of missing information. But no one was prepared to acknowledge the role of the brokers in performance improvement and so the pressure and frustration of the support staff just increased, without any significant improvement in efficiency.

Performance measures must be assigned to everyone in the loop who can have some influence. Take any particular group out of the equation and the performance measures will not generate the correct actions or results and the performance targets will not be achieved.

It is also worth noting that nobody was closely monitoring broker performance in terms of profitable business generation. Yet this was the main way to address the income side of the cost/income ratio. Despite some obvious reluctance to do so, this would have to be addressed at some stage, especially as anecdotal evidence pointed to a small group of brokers who seemed only to generate unprofitable business.

Feedback

This leads us onto the other critical factor of performance measurement, feedback. We do not need to cover this in much detail here because we will make numerous references to this elsewhere (we already have in the PDCA cycle – *see* Chapter 2).

At some stage, the insurance broking company mentioned above was bound to realise that focusing just on support staff was never going to bring about a really significant improvement in the cost/income ratio. The business results would speak for themselves. However, it would need a very strong CEO to start taking the really tough decisions.

Feedback in performance measurement will not happen naturally through monthly figures though. Performance feedback has to be organised and structured so that subsequent, remedial actions are directed at the causes of underperformance and recognise where high performance is being achieved.

Anyone interested in setting up an EPMMS has to be fully aware of the need for feedback and the practical considerations that they will have to face. Are employees ready for honest feedback? Will feedback be perceived as constructive or as just criticism? Above all else, though, to give good feedback on performance you need good performance information systems.

6

Management information systems and people performance

- Management information systems 55
- Where are we now? 56
- Measurement tips – using measurement intelligently 59

MANAGEMENT INFORMATION SYSTEMS

How long ago was your current management information system (MIS) installed? This is a bit of a trick question. MISs are rarely designed as a one-off exercise. In fact, when you come to think of it, how well designed are they? They tend to be designed around the needs of those who produce tangible data. Production managers want production information, sales people want sales information and accountants want to lay their hands on as much financial information as they can.

Once the system is in place it tends to be adapted and changed to suit the ever-changing demands and priorities of whoever is calling the shots. So an *ad hoc*, piecemeal approach to MIS continues.

A production director whom I used to work with received a full printout every day (about 2 inches thick), from the management accounts department, detailing everything he would ever need to know about the previous day's production performance. It included everything from inventory, raw material costs and wastage, rework and scrap rates to production outputs from each production line and associated labour costs.

The amount of effort necessary to set up and maintain this MIS was considerable but it was like a millstone around the production director's neck. It did not inspire him, excite him or even focus his attention on any particular areas. All it did was seem to make his life an unbearable misery.

One Friday night, during a particularly fraught period, we were chatting in his office and both breathing a sigh of relief that we had survived another week, when I spotted a huge pile of these computer printouts on his filing cabinet in the corner of his office. I asked him where he normally filed these and he said he did not file them because, as daily operational information, they had a very short shelf life. He went even further to admit, in confidence, that he had not had time to look at any of them this week!

This was the clearest illustration I have ever seen of data (not information) overload. Because finance teams and MIS experts *can* produce data, they do – by the lorry load – and computers have helped them. These daily printouts were as helpful to the production director as unloading a ton of bricks in his office every morning.

So we come to the whole issue of *producing meaningful management information in a user-friendly format which helps managers analyse, focus and prioritise.* Even when management information overcomes this basic hurdle there is then the secondary question of who has to do what. What does the information tell us about the performance of people rather than a production line or a piece of equipment?

From a people performance perspective, what useful information does the MIS actually provide. Would the MIS be able to produce the range of performances achieved by employees (see Chapter 7)? It is all very well to have a measure of tonnage per person but we need to know which employees are influencing this indicator and to what extent.

On a consultancy assignment once, with a hotel group, I was trying to correlate employees' performance with their length of service. The personnel department could not help even though they had all the necessary service data. So they pointed me in the direction of one of their MIS experts at head office. His initial response was that the company's MIS was now so good that it could produce anything I wanted. He obviously had not anticipated my first request for a distribution curve of employee service periods, because he plainly could not produce what I needed. (As a general point, from my own experience, MISs always have problems taking employee service data and producing meaningful graphs.)

I moved on to a request for comparative performance data. He could produce bar and restaurant figures for any of the hotels in the group but could not identify which employees would be responsible for them. In theory, his system should have been able to produce drinks and food figures for every barperson and waiter because all till receipts were attributed to a given employee number. However, there was no way that this system would illustrate, especially graphically, who were the best bar and waiting staff and who were the worst, based on sales figures.

MISs are not normally designed with employee performance information in mind. Ask any senior manager what information they can get out of their MIS about a specific employee or group of employees and they will be struggling. At best you would be given a simple sales or commission figure for an individual. Other than that they might point you to the personnel department to find out something about their personal employment details.

So who needs to ask for people information and what people information do we need? Perhaps we can consider several dimensions of employee information and how it might help us to analyse and improve performance.

WHERE ARE WE NOW?

Employee retention, stability and turnover

Measuring employee retention is relatively simple, but analysing the causes of staff turnover is a notoriously complex exercise. Nevertheless, staff turnover rates are always a very quick organisational health check indicator. This does not mean that the only aim in life is to have as low a turnover as possible. The aim is to have the level of staff turnover that you planned to have. McDonald's live with staff turnover rates well in excess of 100 per cent and seem to thrive on it. IBM, on the other hand, had a staff turnover rate some years ago of 1.6 per cent and, as a consequence, suffered badly when it had to make large numbers redundant in the early 1990s.

The simplest measure of staff turnover is crude wastage. This measures how much 'churn' there is in the workforce by looking at leavers as a percentage of the number of employees:

$$\frac{\text{Leavers in last 12 months}}{\text{Total employees}} \times 100\%$$

Another useful measure is employee stability:

$$\frac{\text{Employees with >12 months service}}{\text{Total employees}} \times 100\%$$

Stability is particularly useful when there are high recruitment and initial training costs involved. Low stability means much of this money is being wasted.

These measures are also useful for two reasons in performance terms:

- *If staff turnover or stability is not close to what you want it to be it means something is fundamentally wrong with your HR strategy.* Macdonald's are geared up to living with a high staff turnover. Employment policies should be developed to match the level of staff turnover you have.

- How can you develop high performing people if your people keep changing?

Employee productivity

How productive, generally, is your workforce? It is amazing that comparisons of labour productivity usually compare productivity between nations by way of reference to a very simplistic output per head figure, the most obvious example being car production. We hear of the number of cars produced per employee, but this never seems to take into account the relative amounts invested in new technology.

Employee productivity data should also measure potential and comparative human productivity. One way to measure this is to look at what the best employee can achieve as a benchmark (*see* Table 6.1). So, if, in a team of 11 people, the most productive employee produces, say, 15 units out of a total production of 110 (i.e. 13.6 per cent of the work) then, in theory, every member of that team should be capable of producing a similar amount of work. If they all performed at this level then the total output of the team would increase by 50 per cent. We can represent this another way by saying the team is currently only working at 66.6 per cent of its potential capacity.

Table 6.1 Employee productivity and capacity

Employee number	Current performance (units per day)	Potential max. capacity	Potential median capacity
001	6	15	12
002	6	15	12
003	7	15	12
004	7	15	12
005	7	15	12
006	**12 (median)**	15	12
007	12	15	12
008	12	15	12
009	12	15	12
010	14	15	14
011	**15 (maximum)**	15	15
Total	**110**	**165**	**137**

This is very powerful information. It aims for perfection but it is a very simple way of indicating what is possible and, in the spirit of continuous improvement, provides a significant target to aim for.

Employee effort

To balance against employee productivity we have to look at employee effort, an all-embracing term that covers such things as commitment, loyalty, flexibility and sheer hard work. Ask any employee to work too hard and they are likely to look for an alternative employer.

For this reason, it may not be wise to benchmark team performance on the best employee. Any reasonable employer has to ask themselves two basic questions:

- How much can my business afford to pay people?
- What effort can I expect for that?

This requires a judgement – there are no perfect answers to such questions. In reality, the benchmark could probably be set near the median performer (the middle productivity score, say 12 units). This would mean that the total potential capacity of this team would now be 137 units (24.5 per cent higher than existing production) at an acceptable effort level.

This should be used as a target to encourage a better performance from all of those who fall below the median. It is worth noting, however, that in this particular example only five employees have to improve their performance.

Of course all of this information can be produced on a departmental and company-wide basis as well as for specific teams and individuals.

Where could we be?

The three areas of measurement above will give an indication of how well the organisation is managing the performance of its human resource. What it does not really tell us anything about is the future potential dimension. So which of these employees can become our next managers? What can these people contribute outside or over and above their existing jobs?

One other angle not normally covered is the extent to which talent and potential is being utilised. It would not be too difficult to ask each manager to provide a very quick assessment of which members of their teams are working at a level below their potential capability. When these figures are compiled for a complete organisation they may be quite startling.

If we assume that this produced a figure of one out of every ten employees not being used to their full potential we may just accept that this is what you might expect. Not everyone can be promoted to where they would like to be.

The converse argument says here is a resource, being paid for, which the organisation admits it cannot fully utilise. If the figures were, say, two out of ten then this really would be a cause for concern.

A combination of Tools 2, 3, 9, 11 and 12 (*see* appendix) should help you to look at ways of producing these figures.

MEASUREMENT TIPS – USING MEASUREMENT INTELLIGENTLY

We have looked at how people can resist measurement and their reasons for doing so. Having made great efforts to overcome this resistance we do not want to ruin things by using measurement in a way that switches people off. We must use measurement intelligently. That is, we must constantly think about what we are trying to achieve and follow the principles and spirit of measurement rather than have a slavish adherence to the need to measure, *per se*.

So, here are a few tips and tricks of the trade to make sure you use measurement intelligently.

Change measures regularly

This probably goes against all conventional thinking, but why do measurement systems stay the same for so long? Why are monthly management reports always to the same format? When measurement is used repetitively it loses its impact. Also, familiarity breeds contempt. When the same bad figures keep being produced people get punch drunk and start to lose much of the motivation they may have had to do something about them. How many times have you seen a manager who has stopped reacting to poor performance measures and just starts accepting their 'punishment' on a monthly basis?

If your answer to this is that changing measures takes time and effort then it is probably worth that effort. Moreover, if existing measures really have lost their impact then they have become redundant anyway. Measurement is a key management tool in making people think. When measures stop working people stop thinking.

A large retail organisation, like most companies, had a system of regular monthly reports. In particular, the HR team had to produce its own report on people-related data. This amounted to turnover and absence figures in the main in a standard format. This was very comprehensively covered but it lacked impact. To improve this information a summary sheet was included on the front with exceptional performance reported (that is, exceptionally good and exceptionally bad). Depending on the culture, this can highlight the best and the worst stores. But the main point is it changed the main thrust of the report each month. This kept store managers on their toes, not knowing what to expect. They had to take an interest because they could not predict, and therefore become inured to, the report's content.

Less is more – information overload

It is not a particularly new idea but measurement is one of the best examples where less information is better than too much information. Give somebody a one-page report, albeit without all of the fine detail, and there is a good chance it will be read. Give someone ten pages of closely typed detail and it is likely to go straight into the pending tray indefinitely. At best the skim reader will only absorb part of the document anyway.

Information overload is getting worse and we are not learning from this. It is driven by accountants and information technology (IT) people who are either obsessed with data or their ability to generate it. You want information and you want it in a format that gets action.

MISs and people performance

Presentation of measurement – aren't accounts boring?

More thought should be put into the presentation of performance measurement information. It has to have an impact and indicate what needs to happen. Management accounts never help the reader very much. It is a basic assumption that anyone, on the distribution list for management accounts, should be able to analyse and interpret the figures presented to them.

A picture paints a thousand words, so always choose graphics in preference to lists of spreadsheet figures. They make it easier to understand and have more impact.

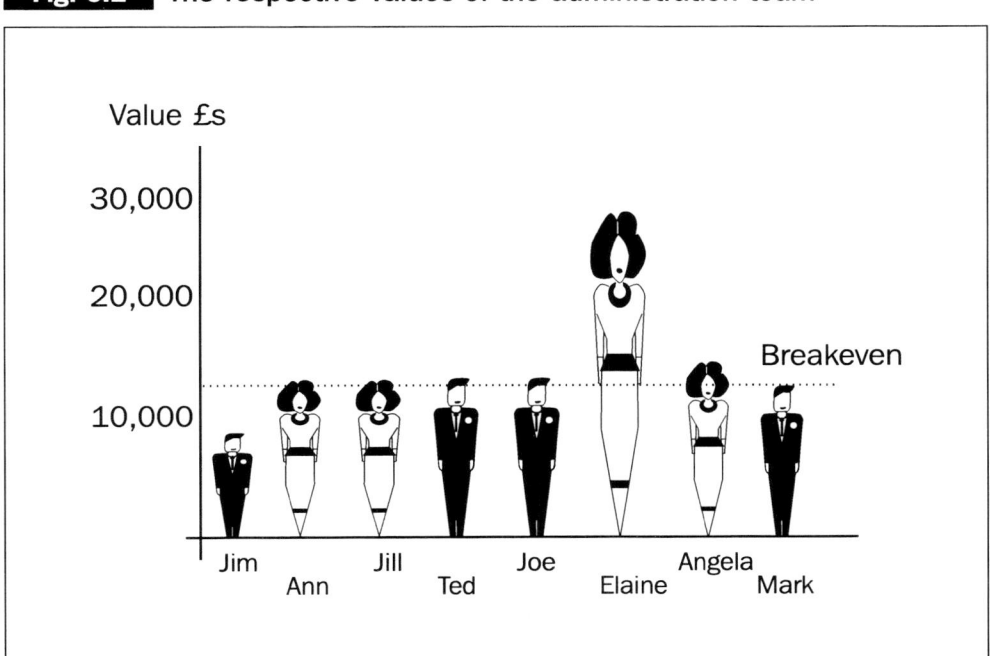

Fig. 6.1 The respective values of the administration team

Figure 6.1 is one idea to liven up people information. This was actually produced by using the percentage contributions of the underwriting administration team given as an example in Chapter 7. In effect, Elaine produces 2.8 times the value of the others. Her value is her cost (market value) times this multiplier. Jim does not even cover his cost.

One final thought. There is a strong argument these days for having some performance measurement and management specialists who develop expertise in analysing and presenting data to produce meaningful and easy to understand performance information for line and operational managers, as well as other employees who have a need to know.

7

The performance measurement proposition

- The performance measurement curve   65
- Managing underperformance   67
- Acceptable performers   69
- Superior performers   69
- Starting to produce the performance distribution curve   70
- Different curves for different aspects of performance   70
- Equal opportunities for maximum added value   71
- Six key elements to maximise individual performance and added value   73
- Installing an employee performance measurement and management system   76

If you or your organisation really want to take performance measurement seriously then there needs to be an agreed framework installed so that everyone is working to the same blueprint. But we are not talking about common appraisal forms or the need for job evaluation. The framework needs to:

- encapsulate the company's philosophy on performance;
- adhere to the principles of performance measurement and management; and
- simultaneously offer a practical basis for implementation.

You might be wondering what wonderfully sophisticated system could possibly fulfil all of these requirements. In fact, it is a framework that has been around for a long time, and it is usually referred to as a frequency distribution curve. For the time being we will refer to it as a normal, performance distribution curve, otherwise known as a bell-shaped curve. One is shown in Figure 7.1.

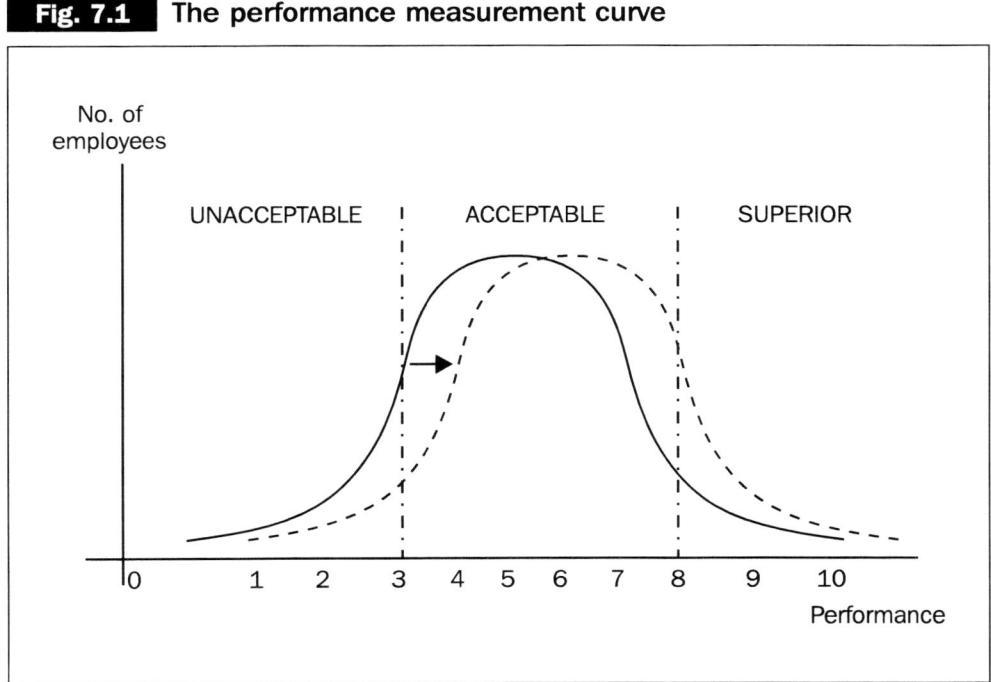

Fig. 7.1 The performance measurement curve

THE PERFORMANCE MEASUREMENT CURVE

But how do we construct such a frequency distribution curve and what does it tell us? If you are not conversant with the simplest of statistical tools then this short explanation should help. However, if you are a statistical genius please do not skip this bit. We are going to revisit this idea to see how it helps in people performance measurement.

If you asked everybody in your organisation for their shoe size the theory of probability suggests that they will range from very small to very large. If you actually charted the range of shoe sizes on the *x*-axis and the number of employees, of each size, on the *y*-axis, there is a very good chance that the curve would look like the one in Figure 7.1. Most employees would have average sized feet and there would be a smaller number, at each extreme, with very small or very large shoe sizes. That's it. That is all the distribution curve does.

We could go further and suggest that, *whatever you measure*, there is likely to be a distribution something like this. If we did it for height and weight it would probably be very similar.

So, if this is a fundamental law, would it hold true for measuring the performance of employees? Admittedly, we have not addressed how to measure employee performance yet. We have not produced a performance tape-measure or weighing scales. Nevertheless, assuming for a moment that we had a way of measuring employee performance, do you believe the distribution of performances would produce a normal distribution curve?

I asked one particular group of managers to score their staff on a simple 1 to 10 basis, just to see if it produced this curve. This was after having already given them guidelines that scores of less than 3 are indicating that the employee's performance is unacceptable and more than 8 is a superior performance.

An HR director, present at the time, was horrified that this was being suggested in a rather cavalier manner without more sophisticated measures being used. I was just about to suggest that there was no real harm in this exercise when a senior manager sitting next to her smiled and said: 'We do this already. Paul is just asking us to put some actual figures on the subjective assessments we have already made.' I could not have put it better myself.

So it looks like the normal distribution assumption is sound. Consequently, the curve would suggest that, in any particular organisation, there are a majority of employees who come to work every day and do a reasonable, or at least acceptable, job. A smaller number at the right of the curve are the superior performers and potential high-flyers and at the opposite end are those who do not even fulfil the minimum requirements of their job. This seems to be a reasonable reflection of reality.

We will keep returning to this diagram throughout this book. For now, though, we will just accept that here is the performance management proposition. First *we have to find some measures which will enable us to produce this curve*. Second, *regardless of the actual shape of this curve, what we are trying to do is shift it*. This is represented in the diagram by the move from the continuous to the dotted line. All we then need to do is work out *how* to shift it.

There is nothing particularly new in this idea but its practical application is, for most organisations, revolutionary. Furthermore, performance deficiencies may not rest with the individual employee, but could equally be the result of poor process or simply bad management. Within every section of this curve there is a multitude of human resource issues. Let us quickly look at each section in turn and see what the implications are.

MANAGING UNDERPERFORMANCE

My usual advice to anyone using the performance curve for the first time is to tackle the underperformers first. This does not mean that an organisation has to become a brutal, hire-and-fire employer. But, by the same token, you should not shy away from the whole issue of underperformance either.

If the effect *we want is a shift in performance then we need to work on the* causes *of underperformance*. First, identify the underperformers and then put some effort into analysing the causes of underperformance. Also, try to distinguish between lack of capability and lack of effort. This is the antidote to broad-brush, scattergun, organisational change initiatives.

As with many things in organisational life, though, what appears to be obvious on paper is less so in practice. No organisation would want to admit that it tolerates underperformance, especially if the shareholders were asking. Yet, in reality, *every organisation does accept a certain level of underperformance*. So why is this apparent paradox so prevalent?

One reason is sheer operational pressure. Recruitment can be a very time-consuming activity and, once a new employee is recruited, there is a natural reluctance to go through the whole palaver again, so soon. Hard-pressed managers, who need every pair of hands available, will put up with underperformance simply because *any* extra pair of hands is better than none. Some managers also follow the principle 'Better the devil you know' but this was never a brilliant management maxim.

Obviously, when the operational pressures relax at a later date, the damage is already done. Not only will the employee now have some rights regarding termination of employment, but there is also a build-up of emotional pressure that tends to make the manager prevaricate about getting rid of them.

Very few managers actually relish the possibility of firing someone. Moreover, if this underperformer happens to work for an ineffectual manager then they may well choose to transfer them to another team rather than become involved in dismissal proceedings.

Not all 'underperformers' are bad employees though. Underperformance may be an issue simply because training is inadequate. Again, operational pressures focus on the job to be done today. This means the time allowed for thorough training is not sufficient to achieve the right standard. This leads to a vicious circle of employee and managerial dissatisfaction. However, like most vicious circles this is difficult to break.

There can even be a culture that accepts underperformance. Some organisations believe employees are always worth another chance or do not want to admit failure. Or they feel that they are sending the wrong signals to their workforce.

Companies such as IBM used to go even further and had a 'no redundancy' policy for many years. However, this led to such organisational atrophy that their policy had to change.

The most startling example of how simply and effectively this curve can be used was demonstrated to me when I received a call from someone who had been on one of my public seminars. He introduced himself as the sales training manager for a large life insurance business. He had attended a large public seminar, which I had run six months before, on the subject of how to use evaluation techniques to focus training on performance improvement.

I had not spoken to him at the time of the workshop, or since, but he told me that he had constructed the performance curve and acted on my advice. He did this simply by asking the sales director for the current sales commission figures for the salesforce, producing the distribution curve and then agreeing with the director where the lower (unacceptable) and upper (superior) cut-off points would be. He was quite ebullient on the phone and the reason for this was that he was ringing to tell me what a success it had been. In fact he quoted me sales improvement figures of up to 24 per cent.

I was obviously intrigued to find out more, so he informed me that he had particularly listened to my advice to always focus attention on the lowest end of the curve first. To this end he had designed a new training programme called the 'Underperformers' initiative'! He sensed my shocked reaction to the notion of stigmatising the underperformers and assured me that most of them were quite willing participants in the programme. They wanted to continue working for the company and had an obvious vested interest in improving their sales and the commission they earned.

Even more interesting was the fact that once the successful figures were publicised he was now getting inquiries from the superior performers on the curve. They were so well motivated that they, too, thought they could learn something to their advantage from the underperformers' programme! So much for the stigmatism of underperformance.

There are no perfect answers in performance management but there are some very good reasons why underperformance should be dealt with effectively, if an organisation wants to aspire to become 'high performing'.

The reason I gave the advice to the sales training manager to focus on the underperformers first is that dealing with underperformers is likely to achieve the biggest immediate payback. Also, underperformers are damaging the business.

This may be through inefficiency, poor customer service or even exposing the business to risk. Either way, eliminating poor performance is bound to have an immediately beneficial effect, so it is worth sticking with it.

Probably the most serious consequence of failing to manage underperformance effectively, though, is that it undermines any attempt to encourage outstanding or superior performance. How can you expect performance improvement from acceptable or superior performing employees when they can see the issue of underperformance being side-stepped?

ACCEPTABLE PERFORMERS

As Napoleon said when asked why he had executed some of his own generals, it was 'pour encourager les autres'. This is the other, beneficial, by-product of dealing with underperformance. When the organisation starts to send clear signals about what is an acceptable level of performance it has two simultaneous effects on the main bulk of the employees. They can now see they that they do not have to carry passengers anymore and, by definition, their own performance has openly been recognised as being of an acceptable standard. Both of these are morale-boosting effects.

Similarly, those who are on the borderline of acceptable performance will be in no doubt as to where the organisation is heading and what it might mean for them if they do not start to improve.

SUPERIOR PERFORMERS

Superior performers are a very different proposition. They are already highly self-motivated. They are more likely to be ambitious. If their performance is to be managed maybe they are just waiting for an opportunity to excel. This could simply be a case of giving them more of a free rein or an opportunity to shine.

In this group there may be reward issues or the redesigning of roles. Perhaps the high performers can mentor or coach the underperformers.

Despite my normal suggestion of starting with underperformance there are also compelling arguments for focusing on superior performers. If these are the brightest, most innovative stars they could be the source of enormous added value as long as their potential is tapped.

Perhaps the biggest question for the largest organisations is: are you getting the full potential out of these people?

STARTING TO PRODUCE THE PERFORMANCE DISTRIBUTION CURVE

Without actual performance measurements, though, all of this is just an academic debate, great in theory but questionable in practice. If we cannot measure performance we cannot manage performance. This was one of our founding principles. So we need to start measuring now.

The best way to start measuring performance is not to be too much of a purist. John Harvey-Jones was absolutely right when he said that 'best is the enemy of good'. If this is a new technology then we have to try walking before we start to run. So a simple measurement system is all we need to get us moving.

There is no better way to start measuring employee performance than to ask managers directly. However, before reading any further it would be a good time to try Tool 1 (*see* appendix).

DIFFERENT CURVES FOR DIFFERENT ASPECTS OF PERFORMANCE

Constructing simple performance curves is relatively easy, especially when we use an 'all-in' score. Obviously things can get much more complicated when we consider how many facets there are to performance and the range of factors that can affect performance. Nevertheless, there is no reason why performance curves cannot be produced for very specific aspects of performance.

Probably the first specific measure to use would be productivity, particularly in repetitive jobs where the only real output is the amount of paper processed or calls dealt with. Just going to the trouble of measuring productivity can, in itself, have some interesting results.

I had just trained a group of insurance underwriting team leaders in performance measurement. They were all used to focusing on the task in hand so I asked them to collect some simple productivity data, such as the number of pieces of work completed by each team member. At a follow-up meeting with one of the team leaders he presented me with a spreadsheet detailing the amount of work completed by each of the eight members of his team in one week. This indicated that one particular employee had produced 28 per cent of the total output. This meant the other seven team members produced only 10 per cent each. He remarked that he always knew she was a good worker but this had really opened his eyes.

Productivity will only help performance so far though. *There is an absolute limit on individual productivity*, which is one reason why we do not hear about Taylorism anymore. Also, if we improve productivity and quality suffers we can hardly call this added value. So, simple quality measures can be collected and they too can be used to construct a performance curve. In fact productivity and quality data can be combined to produce another type of simple but effective performance graph as shown in Figure 7.2.

Fig. 7.2 Employee productivity and quality performance chart

Productivity/Quality Performance chart: scatter plot with Quality on x-axis (0–10) and Productivity on y-axis (0–10), divided into quadrants at 5,5. One point at (3,9) in upper left quadrant; remaining points clustered in upper right quadrant and lower right quadrant.

The data to produce this graph could simply be numbers of completed forms for the productivity axis and error rates for the quality axis. Just to illustrate how to construct this chart, the lone dot in the upper left quadrant means this employee scored a 9 for productivity but turned out work of inferior quality, only receiving 3 out of 10.

If we regard the top right quadrant as the area for acceptable performance those outside this area know what they have to do to improve and get a very clear comparison with their own colleagues.

It is worth noting that, as a general rule, productivity and quality are the main dimensions for producing this sort of chart. Elsewhere in this book we discuss other factors that can influence an individual's performance but, at the end of the day, the *two things that are definitely down to the individual are the effort they put in and the care they take to produce a quality product or service.*

EQUAL OPPORTUNITIES FOR MAXIMUM ADDED VALUE

When you are confident in producing performance curves they can be used to make some quite startling illustrations. Perhaps one of the most startling is to compare the performance of male and female managers.

The curve shown in Figure 7.3 is constructed on the assumption that women and men are equal in managerial ability. So for a given employee population of 100 men and 100 women, say, the distribution curve would be the same for both. From these people we want to select our managers and the ideal minimum performance level for a manager is shown by the dotted line (around 8 on the scale).

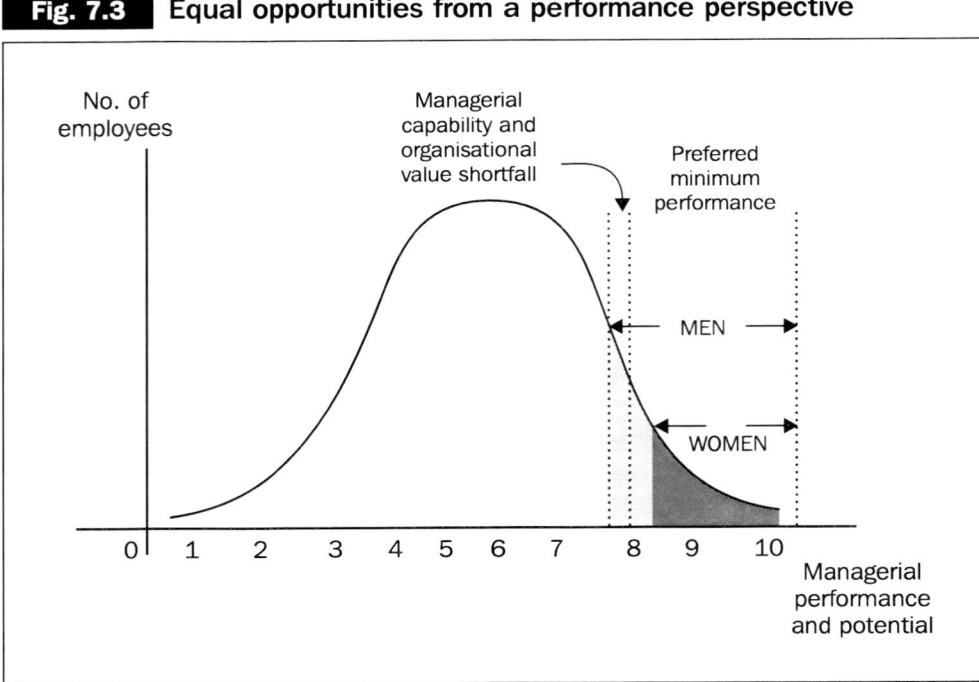

Fig. 7.3 Equal opportunities from a performance perspective

In reality, however, for all sorts of reasons, organisations do not seem to have an equal representation of women at managerial level. This means that they have filled some managerial vacancies with a lower performing man in preference to a more competent woman. This is shown graphically by the grey area below the 'preferred minimum performance' line. This represents a loss in organisational value potential.

If, for now, we accept that performance equals added value, then the whole of the unchecked grey area below the minimum line is how much less value this organisation is producing because of a failure to have an effective equal opportunities policy. Of course, the same argument can be applied to any group of employees who are disadvantaged because of discrimination, intentional or otherwise.

Although, intuitively, most people can see the organisational benefits of equal opportunities the arguments put forward for equal opportunities and diversity policies have often been based, primarily, on moral or ethical grounds. Perhaps there has always been a belief that discrimination results in poorer organisational performance and, hence, lower added value, but using the performance curve can really bring this point home. It would be worth now collecting some initial, simple data to see if your organisation is underperforming because of this.

This is just one fresh perspective on how to achieve improved organisational performance through employee performance measurement. Now we need to look at the key elements that underpin any attempts to improve individual performance.

SIX KEY ELEMENTS TO MAXIMISE INDIVIDUAL PERFORMANCE AND ADDED VALUE

Part of the overall framework proposed in this book is founded on the notion that there are six key elements to maximising an individual's performance. Taking care to ensure these elements are addressed properly will, in turn, add the most value to the organisation. If full attention is not paid to each of these elements then maximum performance will not be achieved.

Processes and systems

First on the list are processes and systems. A business process is the series of steps that turn an input into an output. This could be a manufacturing process turning raw ingredients into a bar of chocolate, the distribution process that delivers it to the shops in good condition or the billing process that ensures the shopkeepers pay the company for their supplies.

Business process consultants always start to draw process diagrams that graphically illustrate the individual steps in the process. What they often fail to do is focus on the actual people who have to carry out each step or activity. This is a grave omission.

It is the processes that start to define the jobs in an organisation. If a brewer introduces new technology and changes the process to take much of the personal touch out of brewing, the jobs that are left are those of low-skilled machine operators, not master brewers.

If we want to maximise individual performance, therefore, we need to ensure we have designed the process to maximise the potential performance of the jobholder.

In the motor insurance market most of us now get insurance quotations over the phone from any one of the me-too, direct insurance companies. Their quotation processes are designed only to provide quotations for the type of customers they want. So, a series of questions appear on the customer service assistant's screen to sift out potentially undesirable business.

When providing a quotation for motor insurance one of these questions might be concerned with whether the car will be used for commercial travelling. If the customer service employee is only given the options on their computer screen of yes or no then there is no leeway for discretion or personal judgement. Consequently this employee's performance measurement is simply limited to making sure all the questions are asked and input onto the screen correctly. After that the technology takes over.

If the process allowed the employee to use their experience and judgement to decide what constituted 'commercial travelling' they may take on a good risk which rigid adherence to the process and system would have declined. To measure performance in this, more judgementally based, role we would have to start looking at the claims experience associated with the business accepted by this particular employee.

Structure

Although second on the list, structural considerations should share equal first with processes. In reality, structure would actually occupy first position on its own.

Whenever a new organisation is created or an existing one takes on a new CEO, the first thing that happens is a fresh look at the organisation structure. This might start with an existing organisation chart or, more radically, the CEO may want to build an entirely different structure on a blank sheet of paper. This would usually be without any reference to processes, even though the theory says this is not, ideally, how it should be done.

What is even worse is that politics, personal friendships and loyalties seem to have as much influence on these decisions as objective and calculated considerations as to what is in the best interests of the organisation. Be that as it may, structure has a direct and significant impact on performance measurement.

Consider again the motor insurance company. Who decides what type of business the company wants to attract? The actuaries, the sales director or the head of marketing? Regardless of who it is the next question is who do the customer services assistants report to? The performance of the actuaries may be based on their ability to predict claims experience while the performance of the sales director could be focused on market share.

At some stage the company wants the best of both worlds – lots of profitable business. However, it is easy to see the conflicting internal forces being set up and causing different functions to 'compete' with each other. Performance measurement has to address this issue head on.

Role

It is the combination of process and structure that determine an individual's role. If the customer service assistants were to report into the actuarial function their processes, position and role would all be focused on delivering what the actuaries want. If the actuaries were now to report into the sales director there would be more emphasis on sales rather than just obtaining business from customers who drive very safely.

Roles can change more often than you might imagine. Certainly any process or structural change will normally have a knock-on effect on the roles of those involved. Even just having a new boss is likely to shift the emphasis in someone's role, in line with the priorities of their new boss.

Awareness

An employee's awareness of their performance requirements and potential is more difficult to pin down. In a university I was working with we were investigating what appeared, on the surface, to be a very straightforward process, the recruitment of new students. In reality it was an incredibly complicated affair.

New student data had to be put onto three different computer systems because of a lack of IT integration. In addition, laborious, manual administration systems were in place which involved several copies of forms being filed in separate places. Everyone was doing their own job to the best of their ability. What they did not have was *an awareness of what influence they could have on the total process*, including how to work with other people in the process to make it work more effectively.

One very simple example was when prospective students phoned up for information. The staff in one section had to write names and addresses by hand on pre-packaged copies of the university prospectus before sending them out. This data could easily have been keyed in once to a database by the receptionists taking the initial calls. This would immediately have improved their performance and simultaneously have provided a more efficient service for students.

Without performance measurement no one could tell them how many prospective students were deterred by slow administration. So employees have to be made fully aware of such possibilities if their performance is to improve continuously.

Capability

Everything outlined above is dependent on the capability of the employees concerned. The receptionists quoted in the example given should be capable of keying in some basic name and address data. However, they may be less capable of analysing where the majority of student applications have emanated from and not understand all the implications this has for admissions policy.

This would require, in practice, installing at least a simple system for collecting data such as 'where did you hear about our university' and a means of summarising geographical data of hometowns.

Considerations of capability should cover every aspect of how an employee performs their tasks. It includes their level of intelligence, their willingness to extend their role and the degree to which their boss allows them the time to do this extra work. Any of these factors can restrict or enhance their capability to perform well.

Organisations that have been following an effective philosophy of continuous improvement for many years reach a stage where the capabilities of even their most junior employees are sorely tested by the increasing demands placed on them. At the far end of this spectrum organisations such as Toyota start to expect all of their employees to be capable of undertaking degree-level education even if they only start as a production line operative. Why? Because it makes good business sense.

Motivation

We touched on some motivational issues earlier when we discussed possible causes of resistance to performance measurement. It is worth reiterating that without seriously considering the motivational aspects of performance measurement, trying to install an EPMMS is going to prove to be a long and arduous road.

Having said that, it would be a good time to look at Tool 5 (*see* appendix) on the effect motivation has on performance.

INSTALLING AN EMPLOYEE PERFORMANCE MEASUREMENT AND MANAGEMENT SYSTEM

Following on from the key elements above we now need to consider how to actually install a robust EPMMS. There are five main steps that should be followed.

Performance measurement

Obviously the first step is to have a system for producing employee performance measures.

The objective here is to produce a measure, or set of measures, that individual employees can own and use as a focus for their improvement efforts. In the early days of setting up a EPMMS the measures may not be perfect but they should adhere wherever possible to the guiding principles of measurement (*see* Chapter 3). Tool 7 should also help (*see* appendix).

If you have not already completed Tools 2 and 3 (*see* appendix) then now is the time to do so. These are described as 'quick and dirty' exercises because they start from the premise that a very subjective measure will suffice to get the system off the ground. This means that they are far from perfect but you can hone and develop the measures as your confidence builds and the credibility of the system is established with your employees.

Performance review

Performance management is not a one-way street. It should be the focus of a continuous dialogue between supervisor and subordinate and any others involved in the same processes. However, there should be at least one occasion per year when this dialogue takes place on a slightly more formal and systematic basis.

Ask any organisation whether they have a performance review process or system in place and they will usually talk about their appraisal or personal development planning system. Sometimes, though, this is purely intended to be a training and personal development discussion with no reference to pay or rewards.

Some organisations, however, discovered after many years that traditional appraisal systems, while alright on paper, rarely delivered anything useful in practice. My own personal experience of a whole range of performance review formats tells me that they are very often blunt instruments. To put some teeth into yours I suggest you look at Tools 7 and 8 (*see* appendix).

Structure/role analysis

While a performance review discussion is taking place, especially if the reviewee is feeling under some pressure, it is very likely that the discussion will turn to a fundamental look at the job, role and activities of the person concerned.

Setting measurable performance objectives will flush out comments such as 'that's all right as long as I have the time to do it', 'everything I do seems to be a number 1 priority' or, a more telling indicator, 'I can only do that if Bill lets me have the information (or whatever) on time ...' A skilful reviewer will not jump to the conclusion that these are just excuses for not performing, even though some of them may well prove to be just that.

Someone with too many priorities could have too big a job and needs to have someone promoted to share the burden, while those who are victims of someone else's failure to perform could be desperately in need of a bit more authority to deal with this issue directly, themselves.

Reviewing where someone sits in an organisation is a complex area involving levels of authority and accountability, reporting lines, role boundaries, personalities and politics, to name just a few of the factors.

All of this can be viewed as just part and parcel of holding down a managerial job in a modern, fast-moving environment. That could well be the case but if you are serious about trying to measure and improve performance this is an area that offers many opportunities for those skilled enough to tap it. We will come back to this in Chapter 14.

Process/role analysis

Similarly, the reviewee's role in relation to changing processes has to be fully understood before attempting to measure and improve performance. For example, if the process for ordering stationery changes so that all orders are processed by one central department, rather than each separate department, then the person responsible will have to impose some rules on the latest times for submitting orders. This could immediately be a source of friction even if it is meant to be more efficient.

One advantage of a process-focused analysis is that it automatically crosses over departmental and functional boundaries. The structure/role analysis will highlight some areas of concern but any resolution of the problems is only likely to be achieved through mutual cooperation.

Process/role analysis, using process flow diagrams, can graphically highlight where someone's performance is undermined by poor performance at an earlier or later stage in the process. It also gives those involved in the process an implicit mandate, more or less regardless of hierarchical considerations, to do something about the problem, or at least bring it to a head.

So a production manager cannot hit their production targets very easily if those responsible for storing raw materials allow damaged parts onto the production floor. Showing what percentage of production problems is attributable to a poor part of the overall process is bound to generate some action by those who need to resolve the problem.

In these circumstances it is difficult for any senior manager to stand in the way of sorting out such obvious deficiencies in the process.

Business focused value analysis

Although last on this particular list, this item is most definitely not the least important. It is the whole *raison d'être* of performance measurement.

We do not want performance measurement for the sake of it. Neither should it be conjured up out of thin air. I was subjected to a performance system myself, once, which dictated that each manager had to have ten objectives set by their boss. Achievement of these objectives would be used as part of the calculation to determine my own annual bonus.

The only reason it was ten objectives was that the bonus points calculation system had been structured that way. It dictated there should be ten objectives, no more, no less. This is not intelligent use of performance measurement and is a ridiculous way to develop an EPMMS. Although several of the objectives set were very important the last few were agreed almost just to make up the numbers.

Performance objectives should be linked to added value. Someone in the business should already have worked out where added value is to be created. This should be set out in the business and operating plan. So, if costs have to be reduced by 10 per cent, the accounts should already be showing these figures and be used as performance targets for each manager. If a manager has to start dreaming up performance measures there is something fundamentally wrong with the EPMMS.

All employee performance measures should be connected to something in the business plan.

8

Performance and added value are not the same

- What is added value? 83
- Double-Glazing 'R' Us 85

WHAT IS ADDED VALUE?

If the subject of performance measurement has moved right up the agenda in most organisations then the subject that just manages to pip it to the post is the whole question of added value. The concept of added value is so important that it is not only commercial organisations that talk in such terms; even not-for-profit and public sector bodies now talk about added value or best value. *The question now is 'if it does not add value why are we doing it?'* This is a critical question whenever discussing employee performance.

The education sector, in particular, is having to address this issue in the face of the increasing use of league tables. For them the basic question is how good is the raw material they work with (i.e. their student intake) and to what extent can they add value through education? League tables should only be constructed on measurements of outputs (e.g. qualifications) with a corresponding input measure (initial academic or intellectual capacity of the students) to show the difference, the true added value, that education has produced.

If they do not address this issue, the educational institutions drawing their students from the less privileged end of society will always look as though they are underperforming. League tables and measures will break one of the fundamental principles of performance measurement if they do not have adequate input or added value measures in place.

Added value is a crucial concept in performance measurement so we had better make sure we know exactly what it is and how we can begin to achieve it. In previous titles in this series (Kearns, 1995 and Kearns and Miller, 1996) a clear definition of added value was set out. In short, added value can only be achieved in any organisation by increasing its output, reducing the cost of output, increasing prices or improving, measurably, the quality of the product or service an organisation provides.

Figure 8.1 is an attempt to illustrate this simple definition of added value. However, it is rather a slippery concept, even though, in essence it is very simple. To gauge added value you first need to know what your existing organisational value is. This can only be assessed in relation to what products or services you produce. This is following the principle of baseline measurement. What is our value now and how will it grow over the next year, three years or even five years?

If your organisation makes or manufactures products this should be relatively straightforward. Your value can be expressed in terms of number of units at a certain cost, sales volume or just profits. At a different level of understanding it could be shareholder value or whatever you choose to value (e.g. brand value, market share). The key point is that everyone in the organisation should know what is valuable. Then they can focus their performance on adding value. We will only know whether value has been added, however, by referring back to the metrics chosen. So did market share increase, have profits improved, what is the average cost of producing one unit?

Fig. 8.1 Added value can only come from a few variables

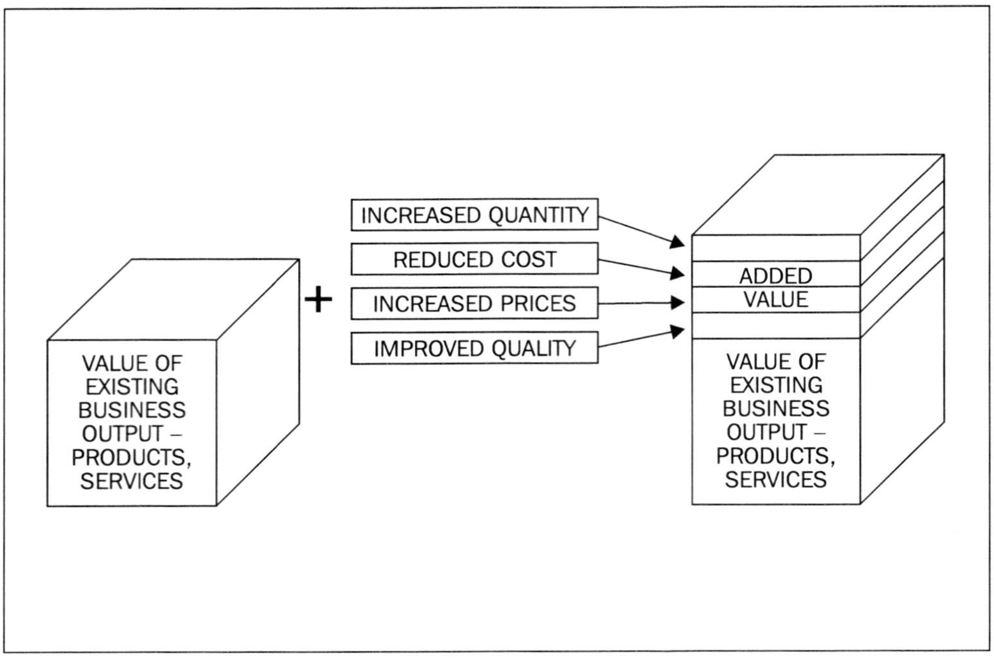

VALUE OF EXISTING BUSINESS OUTPUT – PRODUCTS, SERVICES + INCREASED QUANTITY / REDUCED COST / INCREASED PRICES / IMPROVED QUALITY → ADDED VALUE / VALUE OF EXISTING BUSINESS OUTPUT – PRODUCTS, SERVICES

I show Figure 8.1 every time I run any seminar or workshop, more or less regardless of the particular topic. I also include it in many of the pieces I write. Why? Because *added value is the* raison d'être *of organisational life*. If everyone in the organisation is not contributing to value then what are they doing? They certainly would not be performing. There are several key lessons to be drawn from this definition of added value:

- There are only a few variables worth looking at when trying to gauge added value and they are all highly measurable, in tangible terms.

- Added value is a holistic concept: you cannot guarantee to add value just by focusing on only one variable. Focus just on costs and quality may suffer; this could reduce sales and value.

- Every organisation has to define, for itself, what it regards as valuable. Educationalists must agree what value they are focusing on. For a school, is it academic qualifications or a better citizen? For a manufacturer, is it average cost or profit per unit?

- Added value can always be measured in £s. Even a hospital's value to society is only as much as the output it achieves for a given budget. Society puts a value on this output by funding the hospital. If society *valued* the hospital more it would be prepared to increase its funding.

The full range of levels of understanding can be applied to the concept of added value. I am absolutely convinced that most employees have still only achieved level 3 on this critical subject. Simple proof of this has happened at Cadbury's, the confectionery manufacturer, where they have employed a value management consultancy. It was the consultancy that had to point out to Cadbury's that chocolate buttons were one of its highest, added value products. Intuitively, anyone could have worked this one out. Any parent who buys a packet for their children knows immediately how light the packet is compared to a similar priced chocolate bar. Yet this company had to have someone come in to tell them this and exploit the full potential of this product.

We could spend several more pages looking at added value but we now need to move on and see its relevance in performance measurement and management. We will do this by reference to Figure 8.2. Let us look at this very simple example and then we will see what general principles and lessons we can learn.

Fig. 8.2 Double-Glazing 'R' Us

	Activity/income/cost per day	Performance measures
Telephone canvasser	100 calls per day	Number of calls
		10% sales leads
Salesperson	10 sales visits	Number of visits
		10% conversion
		Average contract price
		£3000
Fitter	1 contract completed	Time taken/Within cost
		Quality/faults/complaints
Average contract price	£3000	
Costs excluding wages	£2400	
Gross profit	£600	
Wages of £100 each per day	£300	
Net profit	£300	
Net added value per employee	£100	

DOUBLE-GLAZING 'R' US

Figure 8.2 is a summary of the EPMMS in a small double-glazing business called Double-Glazing 'R' Us. The measures imposed on the employees by the owner are designed to make everyone perform and ensure the business makes a profit.

There are only three employees in this business: a telephone canvasser who rings potential customers to ascertain whether they might be in need of double-glazing; a salesperson who is provided with leads by the canvasser; and a fitter who fits the double-glazing.

Like most performance measurement systems, this one is based on a combination of activity measures and measures that have a direct impact on cost or revenue. The canvasser has to make 100 calls per day and ensure that 10 (10 per cent) of these lead to sales appointments for the salesperson. The initial canvassing activity now starts to funnel down to the other employees.

The salesperson has to cope with 10 sales visits per day and must achieve a conversion rate of 1 contract per day (10 per cent). The boss is wise enough to realise that they must also include a contract value in the measurement, otherwise the salesperson would have no incentive to negotiate large contracts, hence the added performance measure that, on average, each contract should be worth £3,000.

Finally, assuming this business manages to meet its targets, at the end of the sales funnel, the fitter should have £3,000 worth of windows to fit every day. Again, the boss wants to ensure this work is carried out on time and to the expected quality standard so there are performance measures included as a safeguard against running with excessive costs or customer complaints.

We should also note that, whoever set these targets, the company's accountant would have done the necessary sums, based on these figures, and constructed the business plan accordingly. So, if every employee 'performs' the business will perform. It is a perfect system. So let us assume that everything works perfectly, for the time being.

In this case each employee performs according to the measures set. As a result of this, the figures show that they are each paid a wage of £100 per day and this leaves a net profit for the owner of £300 per day. We can call this the added value to the owner from this business. If we divide that figure by the number of employees (3) we have a net added value per employee figure of £100 per day. Everybody is happy. Like all perfect systems, though, things never work out in practice as smoothly as the most optimistic view would suggest.

Unfortunately, the salesperson at Double-Glazing 'R' Us is headhunted and the replacement, recruited by the boss, only achieves a 5 per cent conversion rate (i.e. one sale every other day). As soon as this starts to happen the net added value per employee figure, shown at the bottom of the table, becomes at least zero (in reality it is more likely to become a negative). Every other day the *net added value per person* figure drops to at least −£300 per day (the cost of wages).

We do not need to spend time calculating the exact figures here. *The main point is that the underperformance of just one member of this 'team' results in the loss of added value from everyone in the team.* Whatever measure we use for performance, and regardless of each individual's actual performance, *one team member can completely negate the performance efforts of the other team members.*

If you are now reciting to yourself the old saying that a chain is only as strong as the weakest link you are absolutely right. This scenario is stating the blindingly obvious. Yet if it is that obvious why do performance measurement systems just focus on narrow individual performance so often, rather than actual added value measures?

The boss cannot replace the new salesperson very quickly or easily so they have to make the best of the situation. Nevertheless, the boss has to explain to the canvasser and fitter why they may have to take a drop in wages until things pick up. Needless to say both of these employees will not take kindly to this suggestion.

The canvasser argues that as she is achieving her performance targets the boss is obliged to pay the same wages as before. The fitter also retorts that it is not their fault that they are sitting around waiting for work every other day.

The boss now realises that the EPMMS system should have had an element of added value measurement in it. Something that ensured every member of the team pulled together. Each employee should have been paid according to *profitable* sales figures. The current system tends to reward effort and activity more than results. So when things were not going so well, all it led to was an awful atmosphere where the employees started to blame each other.

Added value performance measures may seem to be unfair but they force teams to work together. It is the measures that bind them. Also, where each employee works in a different department, possibly under a different boss, added value measures mitigate against turf wars and politics. What gets measured gets done. If the performance measure is measuring the added value of the team effort then the team will add more value.

After presenting this concept to a group of managers from a public utility company we started to discuss their debtor problems (measured by the amount of debt over a number of days). These were supposedly being exacerbated by the technical services department because complaints about such things as leaking pipes and faulty sewers, blamed on the company's' technical teams, had resulted in customers delaying or refusing to pay their water bills. I asked what performance measures were in place and was told that technical services were a completely separate department to the billing department. It was obvious to me that neither team had performance measures that would pull them together in solving the problems.

My suggestion was to set the same added value performance measures for the managers of both the billing and the technical services departments. In practice this meant that the technical services manager should have been given a debtor days target. You can imagine the mixture of shock, howls of laughter and ridicule that I had to suffer having just made such a ridiculous suggestion.

The laughter only subsided when I went on to suggest that if they followed my suggestion the technical services manager would be forced to address the true business problem of worsening cashflow as well as their own immediate technical problems. It would also mean that the manager would have to work hand in hand with the billing manager if their performance objectives were to be achieved.

Just as an aside, as someone who spends a great deal of time helping organisations to evaluate training and development, I am always amazed that team building and team development programmes never address the connection between team performance and organisational added value. Instead the focus always appears to be on intangible factors such as team spirit or team cohesion, whatever that is.

Performance and added value are not necessarily one and the same thing. But it is up to the person setting the EPMMS system up to ensure that they are synonymous. We will cover in more detail later how clever use of measurement can have many, many beneficial influences both behaviourally and organisationally, but let us first look in more detail at the connection between motivation and performance.

9

Motivation and performance – what's the connection?

- Does high morale lead to high productivity? 92

It has always amazed me how glibly business leaders and line managers talk about the levels of morale and motivation in their organisations. The number of times I have heard that 'morale is at an all-time low' in organisations such as the National Health Service would suggest that it is likely to grind to a halt at any minute. Admittedly, it could always improve quite significantly, but it certainly has not come to a standstill. In fact, although the UK spends a smaller percentage of GDP on healthcare than most of its European neighbours surveys suggest that the British people still believe the NHS is an excellent institution that provides a good service.

At a more micro level, who would not agree that there must be some causal connection between individual motivation and subsequent performance? A happy workforce is a productive workforce. This is what our intuition tells us but then we must remember that intuition, at level 1, is the lowest level of understanding. Maslow, Herzberg *et al.* surely only studied the subject of motivation because there was an implicit assumption that better motivation means better business. So, when devising an EPMMS, levels of motivation are bound to be a major concern.

We do not want to muddy the already murky waters of motivation theory here but it might just be worth taking a fresh view of some of our most cherished and deep-seated beliefs about the links between motivation, personal effectiveness and ultimate organisational performance.

Think about your own level of motivation at this precise moment as you are reading. Are you laid back, fired up, curious to know more or quite apathetic? Now try to think how motivated you were 24 hours ago. Were you driven to achieve a particular task or were you working through your in-tray at a steady pace? How much change is there in your motivation levels from one day to the next, or even on the same day?

Now think about your career to date. Have you achieved what you wanted to achieve? Have you reached a particular milestone? How ambitious are you or does that seem to change from one month to the next?

Motivation is a complex area and it seems to ebb and flow like the sea for most of us normal mortals. I often say to conference audiences that I know very little about any person's pattern of motivation, partly because there are so many facets to it and partly because motivation is a very personal matter. We do not want to discuss openly all of the motivational forces that make us do what we do.

Why should we discuss what motivates us? At the end of the day we will normally be judged by our efforts, our actions and our achievements, in short our performance. We might complete an important task on time because we are motivated by pride in our work, because we know one of our colleagues needs us to or simply because we are afraid of the consequences if we do not. These are all different motivators, and they probably combine to drive us to complete the task. But is the organisation interested in the motivating factors or just that the task has been completed satisfactorily?

From a performance perspective, all that most organisations want is effective performance, more or less regardless of motivation pattern. 'Our people are our greatest asset' really is the great corporate lie. Yet, if we genuinely believe that there is a direct causal relationship between how motivated employees are and how effective they are, then we should do whatever we can to ensure that they are highly motivated. Otherwise why bother?

I am convinced that one of the greatest motivators for employees is to be asked to get involved, to be allowed to contribute as much as they have to offer in the ideas they have for solving business problems. This probably does not motivate everyone but I have seen how it has motivated employees many times. This sort of motivator is continuous and, best of all, it comes for free.

Tool 5 (*see* appendix) is intended to test your view of your own particular pattern of motivation. It then goes further to ask whether you believe that your level of motivation influences your level of effectiveness. When you have considered what motivates you, you might want to try it out on one of your colleagues or a member of staff in your team.

A friend of mine, whom I used as one of the original guinea pigs for this exercise, was fascinated by it but concluded that it had resulted in him getting into a complete muddle. Consequently, this is a warning, one which should perhaps be attached to any management tool: use it carefully. If it does not help to improve performance then it serves very little purpose.

DOES HIGH MORALE LEAD TO HIGH PRODUCTIVITY?

Before we move on consider this story. In a large call centre operation which had contracts with many blue-chip multinational companies, one of the monthly measures collected by managers was 'morale'. How do you measure morale, you are probably wondering? Well, apparently you measure morale by guessing what the morale of your team is at the end of each month. Seriously. Each manager was asked to put a morale score down with all of their other monthly statistics. The scale for morale went up to a maximum of 8. Why 8? I do not know.

In the meantime, I was working with this company to help them achieve the Investor in People standard and had quickly discovered that this company was probably not as successful as it thought it was. The one thing a call centre operation has to be is efficient. They get paid according to the number of calls they handle. Therefore, productivity is of paramount importance. I did not sense that this call centre was particularly productive. There was a nice, relaxed, friendly atmosphere, a bit like a student's common room. I decided to try and find out something about productivity measures. The head of HR could not help so I asked to see the finance director.

Motivation and performance

The finance director (FD) was quite young, very bright and a recent addition to the management team. I introduced myself as an HR consultant but quickly added that I was very focused on added value. Then I explained that while everyone was measuring morale maybe they were taking their 'eye off the ball' of productivity. Unusually, for an accountant, he gave me one of the warmest receptions I have ever had. It was as though he had just met the man who was going to release him from the insane asylum.

We sat down and quickly homed in on the key problem. His predecessor left because his MIS was pathetic. The board had no decent information for managing the business. In particular, the system for producing productivity performance had no integrity. He had made this one of his first priorities and he was just beginning to get a clear picture on productivity.

I said that the business seemed more interested in trying to keep the troops happy at the expense of running the business profitably. Furthermore, maybe a small improvement in productivity would significantly improve the bottom line. The FD readily agreed and declared that this was a 'no-brainer'. He had already produced his own calculations to indicate that even a small increase in productivity would have a major impact on the bottom line. Together, at my suggestion, we plotted productivity and morale over the preceding two years. The chart looked like Figure 9.1.

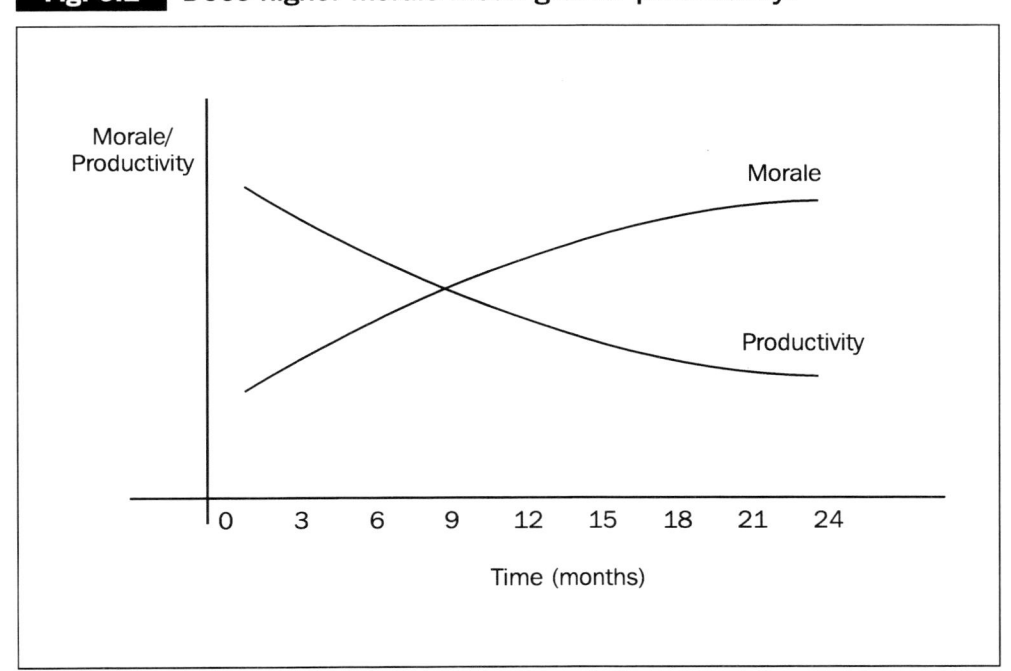

Fig. 9.1 Does higher morale mean greater productivity?

It was only when we looked at the chart that we both were nearly knocked off our feet. The FD said he had been trying to get this message across to the rest of the board but no one was listening. He felt this chart would immediately have an impact. It did. Within a week there was a renewed focus on productivity improvement. Three managers who had been regarded as 'not very good' were found to have the worst productivity records in their teams and were removed.

This is only part of a much longer story. The only relevant point here is that concentrating just on motivation or morale will not guarantee business performance. Motivation may be a necessary condition but it certainly is not a sufficient condition.

Now, before we get too bogged down in this contentious subject, let us move on.

10

Rewarding performance

- Paying for performance 97
- Establishing base pay levels 98
- Performance related pay (PRP) 99
- Fat cats and market rates 100

If you thought motivation was a difficult subject then the problematic area of rewarding performance is even more troublesome. However, I must stress that, as we have already seen, pay is only one of the myriad of factors that influence performance and you can achieve significant improvements in employee performance without any extra pay.

Regardless of which industry or sector you work in, have you ever stopped to think how good the service is in some hotels or how dedicated many workers are in the NHS? These are low-pay sectors. Have you also noticed the really poor service you often get from some relatively high-paying companies, such as some banks, who still treat customers as though they were just an irksome irritation? So, in some low-pay sectors, customers get excellent service and, in some high-pay sectors, the staff just do not care.

Perhaps this should teach us two lessons:

- If you cannot get an acceptable performance for the rewards you are offering never accept poor pay as an excuse from the employee.

- There are obviously many factors other than pay which determine performance, so never look at pay in isolation.

PAYING FOR PERFORMANCE

As an HRM professional, I think it is safe to say that the whole area of rewards, pay, compensation and benefits is so contentious that companies would normally choose to play it safe, if possible, for the bulk of their employees. This is probably why pay and grading systems were traditionally structured around a very formal job evaluation system that seemed to favour consistency and conformity in preference to encouraging greater performance and personal initiative.

The problem with conventional job-evaluated grading systems, despite their name, is that they rarely put the right value on jobs. There is a world of difference between a job description and the way a particular jobholder carries out their role. Two production managers that I used to work with were in identical jobs based on the job evaluation analysis. Yet one manager was hopeless and the other was the best manager in the factory. Admittedly, the better manager was paid a higher salary but to the sterile job analyst they were performing the same duties.

Job grading became popular at a time when the trade union environment in many organisations was a great deal more influential than it is now. This stifled performance rather than encouraged it. The aim for most people when they have a job grade based on job evaluation is to maximise the evaluation points for their own job. Hopefully, this will also mean that they are motivated to improve their performance, but that does not necessarily follow. Consider the case of an employee who told me he was only one point away from a job grade that would entitle him to a company car. He would have done anything to get that extra point but I am not sure an extra special performance improvement was uppermost in his mind.

One of the first, simplest questions that we should ask ourselves is 'do you have to pay for performance?' If you were just about to embark on a new performance improvement initiative would the question of pay be an immediate issue? My own personal experience suggests not. Anyone who has set up improvement teams will know that often there is a great deal of enthusiasm from the participants. Maybe this is because they get a great deal of job satisfaction from working on one of these teams. Or, perhaps no one has ever asked them to come up with ideas before. This can be a reward in itself.

So, in the short term improved pay is not a pre-condition for improved performance, especially for those employees who are only being encouraged to reach the minimum standard anyway.

ESTABLISHING BASE PAY LEVELS

We looked earlier at measuring productivity and individual effort. With traditional job evaluation schemes there was often an assumption made, at the beginning of the job evaluation exercise, that the jobholder must be performing to a satisfactory level, otherwise they would not still be with the company. Anyone with any experience in this field would probably agree that this is a rather dubious assumption. However, it managed to help job evaluation consultants avoid the perilous issue of underperformance.

Surely this must be the starting point, though, for any structured pay and grading system. Some attempt should be made to establish the minimum acceptable level of performance for a particular job. This may not be easy but, somehow, an assessment has to be made, and who better to make it than the manager of the post concerned?

In some administrative or simple operational jobs the amount of work an individual produces should be relatively straightforward. In managerial jobs there are often key performance targets available. Any position where measurement is not so easy will have to rely on a mixture of dialogue and agreed objectives but with a clear intention to assess, on a regular basis, whether the employee concerned is performing satisfactorily.

Once these personal contracts are in place, the company can make a policy decision on what to pay for this acceptable level. The only other decision, then, is to choose how much to pay in relation to the market, whether this is upper decile, quartile or even median pay rates.

Establishing base pay levels is just the start. This level of pay should attract enough people to join the organisation, stay with it long enough and work hard enough for it to meet its business objectives. If everyone was employed on this basis the business should continue to operate at its desired level.

PERFORMANCE RELATED PAY (PRP)

If you are surprised that it has taken so long to reach this particular aspect of performance it is partly because, if you want to get it right, there is an awful amount of groundwork that has to be carried out first. Also this is another of the most contentious areas in performance measurement and management (there are quite a few).

Two of the very first lessons I ever learned about human nature when I worked in industrial relations years ago were:

- Failing to pay employees correctly and on time is rightly regarded as a capital offence.
- It does not matter what you pay them as long as you are consistent. Give everybody a pay rise and everyone is happy. Give just one person a penny more than the others and everyone else is unhappy.

Hopefully you do not need any advice on how to pay your employees on time every week or month. It is the second point that we need to address here. You can use pay to incentivise better performance but you had better make sure you get it right. Below are some questions that you might consider. They can be regarded as the principles that should underpin any performance related pay scheme and you can check whether your own scheme is based on them.

The principles of PRP

- *Do you want a bonus scheme or a performance related pay scheme?*

    A bonus is a 'thank you' that is not expected. It may be a 'thank you' for improved performance or it may just be a general 'thank you' that is paid out of better company results. Either way, the distinction between the two is that one is not directly linked to individual performance, the other is. We are interested here in performance related pay, not bonuses.

- *How will you know performance pay is connected to performance improvement?*

    Your PRP system will only be as good as your performance measurement system. You need baseline measures and targets set that can be linked to improved performance.

- *Is the scheme going to be fair and equitable and will it be perceived as such?*

   First, the scheme should reward the people who perform best with the best pay. However, will the scheme include everybody who should be included or is it just for a small group of salespeople or other clique?

   Moreover, regardless of whether it is a fair system, how can you ensure that it is perceived as such? Fair, not just in the eyes of those in the scheme, but all other employees as well? We do not want to demotivate everybody by paying the chosen few a penny more.

The worst sin for any performance pay system is not being credible. Those employees involved, and those who can view it from the sidelines, must feel that it is a fair system that rewards performance. If it does not actually reward performance or is inequitable then it has failed.

FAT CATS AND MARKET RATES

The American consultancy Stern Stewart, which specialises in generating economic value added (EVA), believes that it is EVA that should determine boardroom pay. In an article in the business section of *The Sunday Times* (17 October 1999), Joel Stern questioned the basis for determining the pay levels of senior people. His main concern is that their pay packages are often connected to making the company bigger rather than to an increase in EVA. He argues that this can actually lead to a destruction of shareholder wealth.

> *Why would managers consciously make decisions that destroy shareholder wealth? The answer is their direct pay is tied to size because larger size is assumed to involve greater responsibilities.*
>
> *Pay consultants use three main criteria to fix direct pay: assets, sales and staff, all of which are size variables. So bigger is almost always better for managers.*

I cannot fault his logic, which he further uses to prove that it is not just size that matters in organisations.

Whatever executive pay is tied to, nothing is more likely to raise the ire of a workforce, or the general public for that matter, than the notion of a bloated board director receiving some astronomic pay deal that they do not deserve. It is a very emotional subject. The privatisation of public utilities, particularly, resulted in some enormous pay rises for board directors who had previously worked (quite happily?) for pay based on civil-service-type pay levels. The usual defence, put up by the Cedric Browns of this world (the ex-head of British Gas who was vilified in the British press for an enormous pay award), is that their pay reflects the market rate for the job they are doing. I think this causes confusion.

You have to pay, by definition, a market rate for any employee, but you expect a performance level as well. The two should go hand in hand but, especially at the senior levels we are now referring to, there are no guarantees. *You have to pay what you have to pay to* attract *the people you want*. The *reward* for doing a good job can only be justified, or not, with the benefit of hindsight.

At the time of writing, Carly Fiorina has just become CEO of Hewlett Packard, reputedly with a package worth between $80 m and $90 m. I am sure Hewlett Packard would not have offered this amount unless they thought they had to. I also believe that if they offered half this amount, but still attracted Ms Fiorino, she would not aim to lessen her performance in any way. Let us not confuse the two concepts of performance and market rates. In her position she could be worth every cent, and much more. I just hope, for her sake and that of Hewlett Packards' shareholders and employees, that she performs well enough to justify it.

Performance appraisal and assessment

- Basic or minimum standard activity   105
- Critical activity and risk   105
- Added value activities   106
- ROI   106
- Non-added value activity   108
- Performance measures hidden in the business plan   109
- When and how often should performance be assessed?   110

Actually assessing someone's performance is yet another highly contentious aspect of setting up an EPMMS. From the employee's standpoint, there is a great deal riding on their assessment – personal pride and promotion chances as well as monetary rewards.

The conventional approach to this has been the typical appraisal discussion. In Chapter 16 there is some discussion of why traditional appraisal schemes do not work very well and Tools 7 and 8 (*see* appendix) offer some ideas on how to do it better.

Here, we are more concerned with ensuring that there is a structured approach to performance assessment and so we need to use another part of the overall framework. The start of this framework is a very simple categorisation of the work and activities an employee is engaged in.

BASIC OR MINIMUM STANDARD ACTIVITY

When you try to assess how an employee is doing first consider whether they, at least, perform to a minimum acceptable level. If you produced some performance data for reward purposes, as suggested above, and know the minimum or median level of work required, then all employees should achieve this level on a regular basis. Otherwise remedial action should be taken with a time limit suggested for improvement.

CRITICAL ACTIVITY AND RISK

Within the basic category of work there is a subset which can be referred to as critical activity. What constitutes critical activity? Perhaps the best working definition is that *if critical activities are not performed effectively you are exposing the organisation to a high degree of risk*. It is easy to identify critical activities in jobs where the consequences of any errors are obvious. So, an operator mixing hazardous chemicals, perhaps, or a nurse dispensing the correct quantity of a drug could be carrying out everyday activities without a necessarily high skill level requirement but which, nevertheless, are critical.

If you really think about it, though, most jobs involve an element of critical activity. At the lowest level we can think of an office junior who fails to pass on an important message, the manager who leaves sensitive information lying around or, at the highest level, the director who fails to insert a particular clause in a contract. All of these expose the organisation to risk: risk of litigation, commercial risk and safety risk.

The fascinating thing about risk is that seemingly innocuous activities can potentially have enormous human and financial consequences. The activity only has to fail once and the full impact of the risk can be felt. Yet, it is very difficult to actually put a value on an employee who performs such tasks exceptionally well. For most of this book we have considered how employees can add maximum value. We can look at areas of, say, cost reduction and measure improvements. Analysing risk is a very different matter, yet equally important in performance measurement. For example, consider the simple activity of a nurse getting a patient to sign a consent form before an operation. How much risk is associated with failing to get a signature on the form?

So, when assessing someone's performance, we should first check to what extent they are minimising, or even eliminating, potential risks. This may actually be worth more to the organisation than looking at added value. The performance of critical activities should normally only be viewed, though, as part of achieving minimum standards.

ADDED VALUE ACTIVITIES

Added value activities are those which rise above the day-to-day needs of the job. Just doing your job keeps the company operating as it wants to, but does not move it forward. Added value work creates a competitive advantage. Any job description can include added value activities (e.g. everyone might look for opportunities to save costs) but usually they are outside the normal range of operational tasks. So, an employee who sits on a process improvement team once a month could regard this as a specific piece of potentially added value work. However, in companies such as Toyota employees have always been encouraged to constantly think about ways to add more value.

There are many other ways to describe added value work: going the extra mile, being creative, devising innovative solutions to the company's problems. However, hoping this sort of work will add value is not the same as actually seeing some performance improvement which leads to real added value with a £ sign.

ROI

Wherever possible added value activity should be subjected to a quick return on investment (ROI) calculation to check whether it is worth doing or not. For those not well acquainted with this calculation it is:

$$ROI = \frac{\text{Gross benefit } (£) - \text{Cost } (£)}{\text{Cost } (£)} \times 100\%$$

In effect, this calculation tells you what return you expect from a particular investment. So, let us put some real figures in to the equation to see how it works. You agree with a team leader that a performance objective is to improve customer retention rates. We will assume that this is a serious objective, that you have some baseline measures (65 per cent of your customers come back to you) and you are aiming to make an improvement (say to 70 per cent).

This equation forces you to ask what real *benefit* this will bring in terms of hard £s. What does this 5 per cent increase look like? One simple way to work this out would be to look at what turnover (say £1 m) and profit (say £200,000) is generated by the 65 per cent, then calculate what the extra 5 per cent is worth (£15,384 profit). There are other figures that we might want to include in the potential benefit calculation, however, such as the reduced costs associated with servicing existing customers as opposed to new customers.

I often refer to the use of the ROI equation in this context as a 'back of a fag packet' calculation. It is not meant to take too much time as long as the figures used are roughly accurate. The intention is to stop you agreeing performance objectives without any clear business measures attached (do not forget the story about the meeting problem discussed in Chapter 3) and to ensure everyone in the team knows absolutely clearly why the performance objective is being set.

Once you have a benefit figure you can ask how much cost will be involved. Will there be a training cost, do you need some new software to track customers, could you even recruit more staff? Let us assume that a new part-timer and an extra piece of software amounts to £10,000 extra cost. We can now complete the equation:

$$\text{ROI on customer retention improvement} = \frac{£15{,}384 - £10{,}000}{£10{,}000} \times 100\%$$

$$= 53.84\% \text{ per annum}$$

It is well worth going to the trouble of producing some figures – it is a very good management discipline. This customer retention idea is either a good idea or not. This calculation suggests it is worth pursuing, where else in your organisation do you generate a 53.84 per cent return on investment?

Obviously this is not the end of the story. Now the detailed implementation plan has to be produced and each member of the team has to agree their own performance objectives which should contribute to the achievement of this return (*see* Tool 7 in the appendix). It automatically generates buy-in, commitment and accountability. It should also flush out resistance and help to anticipate any hurdles which need to be overcome.

Although this example is based on actually achieving a 7.6 per cent improvement (i.e. 5 per cent increase in customer retention from 65 per cent to 70 per cent), as a rule of thumb you should always aim only for a 1 per cent improvement. This is to quickly ascertain whether the ROI calculation gives a good enough return. There are two main reasons for this:

- If you aim to achieve a 50 per cent improvement and you actually achieve 49 per cent, this will be seen as a failure by some. (Internal politics are wonderful, aren't they?)

- Most employees will listen to ideas to achieve a 1 per cent improvement – it sounds feasible.

A lady on a workshop, from an oil company, did this calculation on reducing the cost of producing a gallon of petrol by 1 per cent. The bottom line improvement figures, as you can imagine, were very impressive. She was well motivated to pursue the idea.

You can try the ROI calculation on any performance objective and if you find it difficult producing some simple £s figures you ought to seriously consider whether this was a valid performance objective in the first place.

NON-ADDED VALUE ACTIVITY

Activity that does not fit into any of the above categories is probably a waste of effort. My own experience tells me that, generally, people like to be kept busy. Many are more interested in being busy than they are in asking whether any particular activity is worthwhile.

It might sound rather dangerous to sit down and discuss with an employee what they consider to be non-added value activities. Some people will have pet projects or subjects that they find interesting and want to devote more time to them. So they may try to defend such activity in the face of any questions as to their organisational benefit. Or it might simply be a case of them always reverting back to their comfort zone – the work they understand well and are familiar with.

An HR director told me recently that this sort of discussion revealed up to 1,800 hours of work that was deemed to be non-added value. Even busy bees do not want to hear this. Equally, no one really wants to think that all their effort is pointless and will therefore be unrewarded.

The whole idea behind analysing non-added value activities is to free up some time for an employee. Any time this makes available should be directed towards added value work.

PERFORMANCE MEASURES HIDDEN IN THE BUSINESS PLAN

You may never have thought about it this way before but all performance measures are usually hidden in the business plan. This can best be explained by reference to an incident on an in-house seminar I ran some years ago.

This was with a public sector organisation that carries out inspections. During the discussions, I asked the divisional director what performance measures were already in this year's business plan. He looked slightly puzzled. I said if we look just at costs, for example, how does this year's *planned* costs compare to last year's costs? With a little bit more of a push, he offered that this year's plan was aiming to run the service at approximately 11 per cent less cost than the previous year. It made a really nice change not to hear the ubiquitous, rounded figure of 10 per cent.

I then immediately picked on one of the more junior representatives there, who was involved in inspections, and announced that he would now have to carry out 11 per cent more inspections to meet the business plan. Both he and the head of division took umbrage at my suggestion. The 'inspector' said something to the effect 'nobody told me I had to work harder' and the head of division denied that this is what I could read into his business plan.

So where are you going to find 11 per cent cost improvements from, I asked the director? To which he replied that a whole series of steps were being taken, including new systems, some new technology and one or two savings. Undeterred I asked how much all of this came to (for my fag packet calculation). After a couple of seconds the divisional head said about 6 per cent. 'So where is the other 5 per cent coming from?' I asked. (Have you noticed how people who ask simple questions can be annoyingly persistent?) 'Well I suppose I am asking everyone to work 5 per cent more efficiently,' he reluctantly agreed. The inspector was not pleased. Neither were the rest of the group. This 5 per cent performance improvement had obviously not been communicated.

I turned my attentions to the inspector again and asked him how he, personally, could perform 5 per cent more efficiently. He was, by now, getting quite animated because he was under pressure and said he was working hard enough already. I tried to get him thinking more positively and asked if there were any of his present activities that he could shed. A slightly tortured smile appeared on his face as he pronounced that every Friday afternoon was wasted in having to return to the office for a report-back meeting with his boss. Did this meeting add any value, I enquired? To which he replied that, not only did it *not* add value, but he also found it rather patronising for his boss to still want to see him every week.

We quickly calculated that this meeting took up 10 per cent of his working week. The director, who had been listening intently, immediately agreed that he would sanction the termination of these meetings. The inspector, now with a smile on his face, was left wondering what he would do with the extra 5 per cent of time that he had just freed up.

Performance measurement is hidden in the business plan. Used effectively it can produce a win/win/win situation.

WHEN AND HOW OFTEN SHOULD PERFORMANCE BE ASSESSED?

One serious omission in most EPMMSs is the collection of longitudinal or trend data. This is possibly because of the variety of ways of assessing performance and the simple fact that assessing someone in a managerial position is different to an assessment of them when they were at a more junior level. Add to this the practicalities of keeping track of employees who move around and change companies regularly and it is not too difficult to see why continuous data is not kept.

Despite everything we have covered so far, most of the ideas and practical suggestions tend to be 'snapshots' of performance. They are based on a very short timeframe and relate to a particular set of quite ephemeral performance metrics. These snapshots are very important but because of the problems just highlighted they never actually produce the bigger picture. Some people will shine in a particular position because of their boss or they just happen to be in the right place at the right time. Worse still, the figures may not be a true reflection of their performance (e.g. sales went up for other reasons). What organisations really want is a full picture of someone's capabilities and longer-term potential.

A few years ago a good friend of mine was involved in a senior level assessment exercise for a large utility. This assessment centre approach to selecting future senior managers has become quite popular and often involves a thorough psychological profiling of the candidates. The assessment also tries to view the potential of the candidates from different dimensions such as political nous, leadership qualities and results focus.

As my friend pointed out though, on this occasion, there was no cross-reference made to actual performance ratings for these people in their careers to date, no mention of whether they regularly achieved targets or that they had set themselves and their teams stretch objectives.

An assumption was probably made that the candidates must have been performing well enough to get to their present position. Also assessment centres usually look forwards to future potential and do not dwell on the past. If this is so, then it raises several important questions.

First, as always, the group in question was not totally homogeneous. Some are better performers than others, but this had not been clearly established. Second, were they truly good performers by some reasonably objective criteria or had they risen to their present level through politics or patronage? Third, assessment centres do 'score' people, albeit on psychological or subjective scales. These should be balanced by actual performance ratings in order to obtain the fullest picture of any particular individual.

Performance trend data can be collected and stored relatively easily (*see* Tool 11 in the appendix for a sample form). Records of achievement have been in use in schools for some years now and there is no reason why a similar system cannot work for employees. However, always choose simplicity in preference to sophistication.

12

Key people – critical performance

- Spotting key people 115
- Developing key people 116
- Succession planning 117
- Retaining key people 118

SPOTTING KEY PEOPLE

Contrary to popular belief all men are not created equal (and neither are women for that matter). At least from an organisational viewpoint they are not. Not only do some employees perform much better than others but some also hold down positions of much greater potential value. In extreme cases, certain people hold such key positions that their performance is absolutely critical to the continued success of the business.

Obviously, the more senior an employee then generally the more likely they are to be key people. However, at certain times in the life of any organisation, some positions become the key to future success. Sometimes it is the head of research and development, perhaps, in pharmaceuticals or IT, or it could be marketing, as in the case of the recently appointed marketing director (MD) at Marks & Spencer who is trying to completely rebuild the company's brand image.

Such people represent both sides of the performance coin simultaneously, value and risk. Excellent performance will help the organisation achieve much greater success but their failure to do so will have an equally deleterious effect.

Apart from one or two really key players there may well be many more key employees in an organisation that do not stand out as such. What about the receptionist that all the customers seem to love? Maybe the maintenance fitter who is the only one who knows how a particular machine works? Or the manager who is the only one left, of the original project team, who put the new system in place? You could do a lot worse than try to find out where these key people are. Furthermore, what risk is there of them leaving and not passing their expertise on?

The criticality of certain employees is often underestimated. This was vividly illustrated when I was working with an oil company and was drawing flow diagrams to show how their key people fitted in. One of the key players was a 'supply manager', the person who decides how much oil has to be turned into how many different products, based on sales forecasts. In effect, this person balanced the business's total supply and demand.

Of course, this person was already regarded as fulfilling a very important function but the various flowcharts we produced were like drawing a motorway network, with *all* roads leading to this particular supply manager. The HR director present remarked that he had never fully appreciated just how important this position was.

We then discussed how well this employee was performing and, as the discussion developed, the worried look on the HR director's face deepened. This supply manager was an awkward character, apparently, very unpopular and very difficult to work with. To make matters decidedly worse he was becoming paranoid about losing his job in the face of impending redundancies throughout the group. His personal strategy for preserving his job was to withhold as much information as he could from colleagues in a futile attempt to make himself indispensable. As the months wore on he was even suspected of becoming quite unstable! The HR director made a note to put this matter among his list of top priorities.

DEVELOPING KEY PEOPLE

Another perspective on this particular aspect of performance is the increasing interest in leadership and the development of leadership ability. In a survey carried out in 1998 ('The value of training in the era of intellectual capital', The Conference Board, reported in the American journal *Training*, March 1998) leadership development was deemed to be the most important type of training and development. As many as 92 per cent of the respondents cited this as the most important category even though only 18 per cent of companies tried to measure the ROI on it. This is good evidence of people who are quite happy working at level 1 understanding. They intuitively feel it is important but they have not bothered to work out how important.

This is a brilliant illustration of the lack of logic, dare I say stupidity, which bedevils the world of developing employees to improve their performance. If leadership is important it is important because it can potentially add or reduce value significantly. Take a marketing director and ask the question how much difference would an improvement in leadership ability make in their role. A better leader might try to stay ahead of the competition in product development. Having better leadership qualities they could spur their team on to get product development times reduced, or a higher percentage of successful products launched. If improving their leadership ability does not lead to something like this then why bother trying to develop them?

So, let us put the logic of those who say it is important to the test. Assume that leadership development leads to a mere 1 per cent improvement (our rule-of-thumb ROI target) in how the marketing director performs. To put a £ sign on what this means we can just take a view on how much this position contributes. How about taking a 1 per cent increase in market share: what would this be worth? In a £50 m market, generating £5 m profit then simple logic says a 1 per cent improvement is worth at least £50,000 per year in extra profit. Over a minimum of three years this is worth £150,000. Even at the 1 per cent performance improvement level this is worth having. So, how much time, effort and money is it worth putting into leadership development?

The joke is that most leadership programmes will never set these targets for their participants. The participants were probably never assessed individually on whether they really needed to become better leaders, whatever that means. No one will ever connect up the two. The actual time allowed for the programme will be a few days and no one will follow up to see whether their leadership talents have been developed or, more importantly, whether their actual performance has improved. If the organisation needs 'better leaders' then they will gauge whether they have got better leaders by measuring what they can measure, which is just attendance on the programme. This is definitely *not* a measurement of leadership but it is what happens when we apply different (or no) principles to improving the performance of key people.

SUCCESSION PLANNING

Development activity is also normally focused on providing the managers and leaders of the future. Although succession planning is certainly not a very exact science it does not stop organisations trying to do it. What they usually fail to do, though, is track whether the scheme is working or not.

If you wanted to gauge whether your succession planning is working effectively what are the questions you would need to ask? How about:

- How many managers, at a particular level, do we need in five years' time?
- What is the performance distribution of the current set of managers?
- Can we develop a set of future managers who can perform better?
- Can we put in place a performance measurement system that that can indicate this improvement?
- What is the potential added value/risk of not having the right calibre of managers?
- Which key positions are absolutely critical and must be filled satisfactorily and on time?

Notice that we must ask the performance questions. Measuring just numbers of managers at a particular level tells us very little, if anything. Some organisations are starting to ask these questions and put in place simple measurement systems to gauge effectiveness. Without measures it is amazing how far off track succession planning can get.

At an in-house event with a large pharmaceutical company there was fierce opposition to my idea of trying to measure 'succession planning' because it was regarded as unmeasurable. I imagine there was also resistance because the 'succession planners' did not want to be held accountable.

I suggested that if there was no measurement 'system' in place the least we could do was to hear some anecdotal evidence about the effectiveness of the present scheme. To kickstart the discussion I asked who was the last senior manager to have been moved around as a direct result of succession planning. This happened to be a German who had been transferred to a position in Paris. So I asked for anecdotal evidence of how this move had panned out. The simple answer was that it had not. His wife had not settled and he was not very happy. In addition, the French did not seem to take to him at all.

At this stage someone else chipped in that this particular manager had great potential but on his last move he had ruffled so many feathers that he was moved on again very quickly.

Being the very affable person that I am, I posited that perhaps we had picked on a very bad example to justify the succession planning process and suggested we pick another example. To this, someone started talking about an American who, like the German, was being moved regularly to develop their career and groom them for a senior position. This person had also not found moving globally very easy. Worse still, there were many stories questioning whether this particular person performed as well as had originally been thought. We quickly moved onto discussing someone else.

After several more stories, all of which were good examples of where the succession planning scheme had *not* appeared to work in either the company's or the individual manager's interests, the group of people I was talking to seemed to lose any confidence they may have had in the scheme. The recriminations then started (it was a very formal, blame-type culture) with comments such as 'I told them not to send Gunter, to Argentina, it was never going to work'!

The simplest approach to measurement had painted a very unfortunate picture. It was now up to them to revisit their succession planning scheme. The intuitive approach, that moving people around had to be a good thing to do, was not a good foundation. But then level 1 understanding never is.

RETAINING KEY PEOPLE

Succession planning is one thing; making sure you hang onto the key people you need is another. One large tobacco company actually set its HR team a target of retaining certain key people and they had measures in place to check whether this was happening.

We have looked at all of the aspects of planning improvement, having targets, measuring staff turnover and using simple measures to gauge performance. There is absolutely no reason why any organisation cannot have a simple measurement system in place to regularly review whether it is managing to retain its key people.

Part 3

The strategic perspective – developing an employee performance culture

- 13 A strategic perspective on performance measurement 121

- 14 How structure and process affect performance 129

- 15 Connecting performance, knowledge management, and human and intellectual capital 141

- 16 The role of human resource management in performance measurement and management 149

13

A strategic perspective on performance measurement

- Hurdles towards high performance 123

A strategic perspective

If you do not regard your own organisation as 'high performing', or you are just new to the subject, you cannot expect to make much progress too quickly without adopting a strategic perspective. Hopefully, the issues raised in the earlier chapters of this book will already have alerted you to some of the problems, hurdles and pitfalls that you are likely to encounter along the way.

You can still achieve some significant, albeit short-term, improvement through tightening up performance management and using better performance measures. However, as this is essentially a task-focused approach, it will never achieve the gains that a fresh, strategic perspective can offer. A new strategy to instil a high performance culture should be the first hurdle – not the last.

HURDLES TOWARDS HIGH PERFORMANCE

Ideally, you should only embark on installing an EPMMS having considered it from this strategic perspective. So what exactly does adopting a strategic perspective mean? This is a tough subject but here are some guidelines to help.

Figure 13.1 illustrates the number of hurdles that have to be cleared in order to become a high performing organisation, and the order in which they need to be jumped.

Fig. 13.1 Hurdles towards high performance

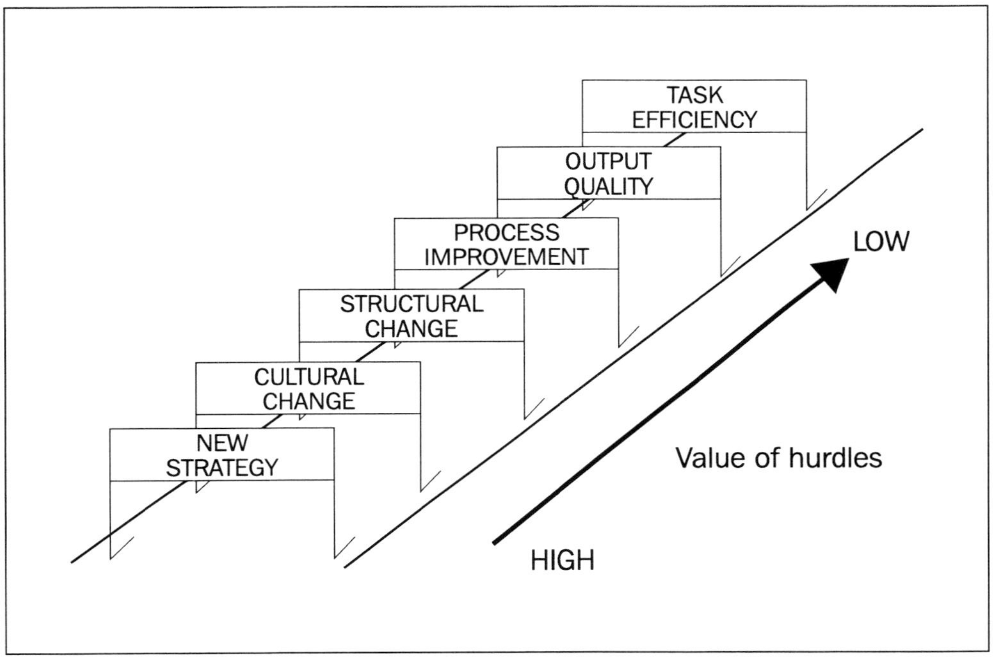

The highest value activity, assuming it is done well, is the formulation of a new strategy for the organisation. Let us assume this is focused on increasing market share through excellence in customer satisfaction. This in turn will lead to questions concerning the culture of the organisation such as 'are we really customer focused and do our employees want to delight our customers?'

When these issues have been considered, the organisation will inevitably have to be structurally changed to become more customer-focused. This could include setting up a customer services team, headed up by a new customer services director. It could also involve moving or reshaping other departments and functions.

Once the new structure is in place the processes that the business uses must be redesigned to give a better and more efficient service to customers. This could be something as simple as introducing a single helpline phone number to deal with all customer enquiries or complaints.

Only when all of this work is done should there be any serious and prolonged attempt to improve output and quality performance. Using a silly example to make a point, there is not much point holding quality circle team meetings or setting up performance improvement groups when the teams themselves are going to be restructured and the processes redesigned.

Similarly, what is the point of installing an EPMMS that tries to improve task efficiency at the lowest, individual level before the role of that individual is clearly defined by the revised organisation structure and new working processes?

In most real-life situations there will be activity on all of these fronts almost simultaneously. While there are discussions taking place about restructuring there will still be efforts made, at an individual level, to improve operating efficiencies. Just because this happens in practice does not mean it is the best way to do it.

These hurdles represent a series of steps for anyone wanting to set up an EPMMS. The only winner of the hurdles race will be the one who jumps them all in the right sequence, even if they do take a few knocks along the way.

We will look in more detail at the interrelationship between strategy, structure, process and employee performance in Chapter 14. For now we just need a broad understanding of how to address each of these elements.

Checking business strategy

The first questions for any initiative or project will always be 'why are we doing this?' and 'what are we hoping to achieve?' The answers to these questions have to come from the business strategy, assuming there is one. If you cannot find something that looks like a coherent strategy in your organisation then an alarm bell should immediately go off in your head.

Strategies are not always clearly expressed in writing so the next option is to ask the CEO or MD for a succinct version of the current business strategy. In this document or conversation you should start to get the feeling that the organisation's strategy is going to stretch everyone if it is to be achieved. If you do not get this feeling, but believe the strategy is a 'default' strategy (otherwise known as business as usual), there should be a serious question in your mind about whether there is a need to develop a new EPMMS.

What you need to see or hear is a clear case for introducing an EPMMS where it has been decided that this is the only way that the business strategy can be achieved. In simple terms, maybe the business is going to try to reduce staff costs by 10 per cent while growing the business by 5 per cent. In effect this means that staff productivity may have to increase by up to 15 per cent.

Alternatively, the company may be fundamentally restructuring its offering to its customers, say from providing them with boxes of technical equipment to providing business solutions. Here the need for performance measurement is very different. The old ways of thinking and working have to change and therefore the old performance requirements, and their measures, will have to change accordingly.

Is culture a real obstacle?

Some organisations have a high performance culture; others do not. Some American corporations, in particular, have no problem driving up performance and offering concomitant rewards to those who achieve, even to the extent that they will happily allow sales people, for example, to earn more than the CEO.

Most organisations would now say that they are managing employee performance and they, too, tend to reward obvious cases of superior performance. That does not necessarily mean that they have a performance culture.

In the UK we are getting used to seeing league tables for sectors where they never existed before in the public sector. Hospitals, schools and other public sector bodies now focus on performance measures. They may be imposed, such as hospital waiting list times, but what gets measured gets done. Even this, though, is not necessarily developing a performance culture.

A performance culture is first and foremost an organisational state of mind. If it is genuinely in the 'culture' it will influence all aspects of the organisation's HR strategy (*see also* Chapter 16). Job descriptions, people specifications and recruitment advertisements will spell out performance requirements. Reward systems will be geared to rewarding performance. Underperformance will not be tolerated. Ideas and innovation will be encouraged from everybody and, year on year, the performance improvements will be manifest in the organisation's results.

Anything less than total commitment to a performance culture will result in limited commitment to continuous performance improvement.

Structural and process changes for performance improvement

While culture is difficult to pin down the same cannot be said for structural and process changes. Figure 13.2 tries to represent, very simply, the complex subject of organisation design. It is a blueprint for designing an organisation from scratch. It also illustrates, in theory, how an overarching vision and mission dictate the direction in which the organisation is to be driven.

Fig. 13.2 Business direction and employee roles

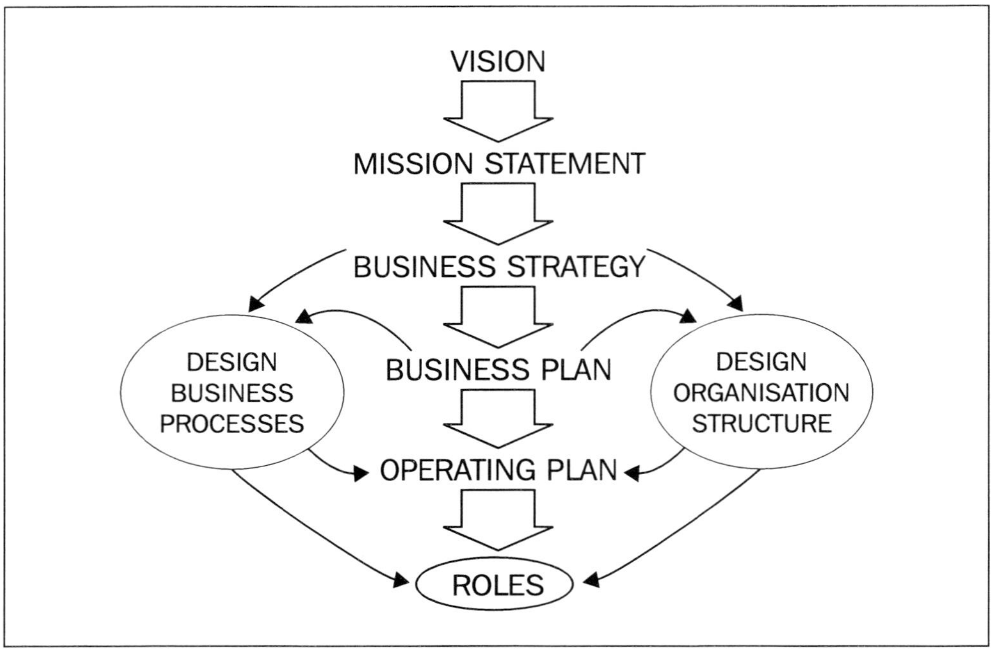

```
                    VISION
                      ⇩
              MISSION STATEMENT
                      ⇩
              BUSINESS STRATEGY
         ↙          ⇩          ↘
   DESIGN       BUSINESS PLAN     DESIGN
   BUSINESS         ⇩          ORGANISATION
   PROCESSES    OPERATING PLAN    STRUCTURE
                      ⇩
                    ROLES
```

Translating vision into reality is dependent on producing an effective strategy which, in turn, leads to detailed business plans and operating plans. Moreover, any change in vision or mission will mean a change in business and operating plans and, by default, the roles the organisation needs.

From an employee performance perspective, we are particularly interested in how an employee's role is connected to business drivers. Organisation structures and processes have to be designed to ensure the organisation can perform efficiently and effectively. They are part of the mechanism for turning vision into reality. Get these wrong and you get the wrong roles. With the wrong roles the people and the organisation underperform.

Unfortunately, while the theory is fine on paper it often does not happen so well in practice. You can probably count the number of visionary business leaders on the fingers of one hand (I bet Bill Gates and Richard Branson are in your list too).

In reality, no one can accurately predict the future so visions, missions and even strategies can prove to be meaningless or shown to be totally off course. It is not surprising that mission statements are often no better than what the IT industry calls 'vapourware' (nothing ever materialises). Human nature being what it is, what CEO wants to tie their colours so tightly to any particular mast when they know they might later be judged accordingly? This is understandable, but it means no one will be accountable for anything.

Consider a chocolate manufacturer that has a vision that the future of confectionery lies in developing chocolate ice creams in addition to their traditional range of sweets. There would be numerous decisions made to help this become a reality but at an operational level we could immediately anticipate role changes. Will the existing sales force have to sell ice creams? If so, how will they carry their samples? Will they have to visit different types of customers and convince them to make room for a new or additional refrigeration unit? These sales people are not just order-takers. They will have to break new ground and might, for the first time, experience real resistance to their products.

Although this is a simple example it highlights some key points. Change any part of the business planning process and you have an impact on employee roles. *The performance indicators for these roles should be clearly visible in the business and operating plans* (e.g. number of new ice cream bars to be sold in year 1).

Just as important, if less obvious, is that a lack of clear and determined vision will lead to unclear roles. Imagine the impact on the sales force if the launch of chocolate ice cream bars was unsuccessful. Not only would this dent their confidence but also, if the organisation then pulls out of this market altogether, reduce their motivation for the next 'new' product launch. It may even lead to a more generally jaundiced view of new initiatives, full stop.

Output, quality and task focus

Most of this book covers the last two hurdles in some detail. The examples given often relate to encouraging employees to do more, to improve the quality of their work or at least to achieve a minimum performance standard.

If this is all your EPMMS does, it severely limits the value it can add. What do you do with the superior performers when they are doing everything expected of them? How can you ask them to contribute ideas if their manager does not want to listen and there is no system in place for ensuring good ideas are implemented?

About four years ago I had a call from Marks & Spencer. They were trying to generate creative and innovative thinking in relatively senior managers by putting them on – yes, you guessed it – a creativity and innovation course. (Why do so many companies think a course is the answer to everything when it is so obviously not?)

The course was not producing results. Surprise, surprise. Maybe, I suggested, this was because the board did not have a vision of a highly creative and innovative company. Therefore, they were not really interested in developing creative managers and would probably not know what to do with any innovative ideas they might generate. Who can say whether this programme improved creativity or not? The market, that's who. It was no surprise to me when M&S started suffering recently. There was no creative culture at M&S and that has been a significant contributor to its underperformance. Who could have convinced the board at that time, though, how misguided M&S were and the disastrous consequences that not changing their culture would incur?

How structure and process affect performance

- Structural change 132
- Process change 133
- Simultaneous structure and process change 135
- Matrix organisations 135
- The office equipment company 136
- Five phases of performance improvement through process redesign 139

Most of this book has looked at ways and means for improving individual performance levels. However, we have also made passing reference to the notion that no employee, team or department is an island. Everyone is linked through the organisation's structure, systems and processes. So to really understand how to create high-performing employees we need a very high level of understanding of the complex relationships between these different constraints and forces. This requires an understanding at least at level 6.

When a new organisation is being set up, or a company builds on a greenfield site, there is an excellent opportunity to design the perfect organisational structure and processes. There are no constraints placed by considerations of length of service, interdepartmental politics or demarcation. Equally there is no historical baggage to offload.

Unfortunately, not every organisation has the luxury of building from the ground up. They have existing structures and processes that cannot be completely demolished, especially as the operation cannot shut down for long enough to enable this to happen.

Organisations are developing and evolving constantly, sometimes in overt, explicit and structured ways, with a new organisation chart, for example. At other times they change in an *ad hoc*, piecemeal fashion, almost insidiously. Someone gets seconded to a project team, their role changes, maybe they do not return to their old job. A new senior manager has the ear of the CEO and starts to create an empire by stealth.

Organisations are like bridges: they were designed for a purpose, in a particular time and context, for a particular set of circumstances. The old Severn Bridge is a good example of this, built in 1966 to cope with traffic volumes which have since been far exceeded. Times move on and as they have to carry heavier traffic they have to be strengthened. A few new struts might be needed to shore up certain parts of the bridge. A bit of new tarmac might cover up a few holes that have appeared on the surface. On occasions this strengthening work becomes so fundamental to the continued integrity of the structure that it has to be planned as part of a complete overhaul. Very rarely does this strengthening work address the real issue that the bridge has become obsolete.

Actually, what is really required is a complete demolition of the old bridge and a totally new bridge should be constructed, designed for the purpose of coping with a very changed world. For obvious reasons, no one is very keen to do this. It is very costly and where would the traffic go during the demolition and new construction phase?

STRUCTURAL CHANGE

I know several large companies which I have worked with over a period of years which have changed their organisation charts approximately every three or four months. We can probably interpret this as being a reaction to swiftly changing market circumstances. Whether this rate of structural change is absolutely necessary or not, though, is open to debate. Of greater concern is the way in which such structural changes are designed and implemented.

It is relatively easy to draw an organisation chart and play around with a few positions on it. Yet every time a change is made it fundamentally alters the equilibrium of the organisation. Promoting someone, or giving someone a new boss, alters working relationships and the implicit 'personal contracts' that underpin such relationships. A career counselling company I once worked for used to say 'new boss, new job'. This is so true, even if the 'job' itself is not supposed to have changed.

New bosses have different priorities; they want to prove themselves, put their particular stamp on the position. They may set higher standards or be more demanding. They will have different relationships with colleagues in other functions.

All of this has an impact on performance which can be positive as well as negative. The new order often leads to fallout, where employees who feel their talent is not recognised decide to move out. Employees who had a boss who was also their mentor may now feel out in the cold. Equally, the 'winners' from the structural changes get a new lease of life. The actual practicalities of handling such changes used to amount to a new job description from the personnel department. Life carries on, but is performance being maximised?

An organisation that is prepared to chop and change its structure frequently is in reactive rather than strategic mode. Surely, in most companies, a clear view of where the organisation is heading, with some contingency built in, will produce an organisation chart that should last at least for the life of the current operating plan, if not the three-year business plan.

A more uncharitable view is that the 'architects' (*sic*) of piecemeal restructuring do not fully appreciate the impact that these changes can have. Taking struts from one part of the bridge to shore up other parts is not to be recommended. It continues to happen because nobody quantifies the potential impact of the new stresses and strains that are being introduced into the organisation through poor design modifications.

The proponents of downsizing seemed to suffer from tunnel vision (no pun intended) in this respect. It is easy to downsize by getting rid of people and showing an immediate improvement in the bottom line through a reduced salary bill. Where, though, are the corresponding figures in the accounts for the inevitable loss in human capital that will result as a consequence? The bank that sheds managerial staff, for example, perhaps only sees the true, net results of their actions as the bad debt ratio rises at a later date.

PROCESS CHANGE

The other way to view organisational change is from a process perspective. Before we do this though let us just stop for a moment to get a better understanding of what processes are and how important they can be.

There are several key things to learn about processes:

- Processes are a sequence of activities that turn inputs into outputs. The cake-making process involves every step from buying the ingredients through to mixing them and then baking the cake. Every organisation employs numerous processes.

- It is the processes, their efficiency and effectiveness, which drive the value chain. At each step in the process value is added. So the employees at each step in the process can be seen to be adding value. The remarkable thing about mapping processes is that it enables us to analyse whose performance is critical and we can also identify where any particular process is failing.

- Some processes do not add any value. Perhaps the best example already used in this book is the process for generating data that nobody uses. Any process that does not add value is not a worthwhile business process.

- Value is always made tangible; it is not a nebulous concept. Better processes mean that the organisation can produce more of its goods and services, or reduce their costs, or improve the quality of the product or service. All of these improvements will surface in the company's results as measurable added value at some stage.

- Employees need to work within effective processes if they are to be able to perform effectively. Similarly, employees need to work within efficient processes if they are to be able to perform efficiently. One only has to spot a queue at the photocopying machine to see the veracity of this statement.

Despite the essential wisdom of exploring organisational performance from a process viewpoint it has to be said this is a much newer idea than straightforward structural thinking, especially if we consider the following quote from a leading process re-engineering expert, James Harrington.

> *There was one major quality breakthrough in the 1980's ... it was the realisation by management that the business and manufacturing processes, not the people, are the key to error free performance.*
>
> (Harrington, 1991)

Harrington's observation is very telling, in more ways than one. First it attributes the focus on 'process' to the total quality revolution, which I think is correct.

Organisations that have relentlessly pursued improvements eventually reach the conclusion that taking a fresh, fundamental look at their business processes will be the source of the next step improvement.

At a session with a group of international managers from a very large multinational, I asked a Japanese delegate how long it took the Japanese to realise that the process is the key to continuous improvement, to which he replied 'about 25 years'.

What Harrington is saying, in short, is that if you get the right processes you will get error free performance, more or less regardless of the people who have to operate the process. This is where, I believe, Harrington and the business process re-engineering movement are wrong. You cannot divorce the process from the people or vice versa. In a hospital there is a very simple process for getting consent forms signed but if the nurse or administrator forgets then the form is not signed. Harrington would probably argue that this is an example of failure to control a process, which is true, but it does not alter the fact that even the simplest processes are at the mercy of the human factor.

Without dwelling too long on this point the main issue here is that process does play a significant part in individual, team and organisational performance. If the process is working properly we can be assured that everyone in the process is performing. So the design and control of processes is key.

Business process re-engineers would always want to blow up the old bridge and design a brand new one. The actual term 're-engineering' suggests something fundamental rather than playing around with minor modifications. The Harrington school of thought, though, seems to ignore the fact that the organisation's employees have been working with the old processes for some time. They like them, they understand them, they know their failings and how to bypass the process if necessary. Their part in the process is tied up with their attitudes and behaviour.

The customer complaint process may have originally put the salesperson in the firing line. If the process changes so that the service engineer has to deal directly with an irate customer, the old excuse of 'you will have to contact sales' is no longer acceptable. How much attitudinal and behavioural change will be needed to transform the service engineer into this new customer-centred animal?

Just as with structural changes, any process change has an immediate impact on performance. Hopefully, the new processes will be more efficient and effective than the old ones. Even if they are on paper, it is down to the employees themselves to make them work and add value.

SIMULTANEOUS STRUCTURE AND PROCESS CHANGE

In theory, if you want to redesign your organisation, you should look at processes and structure at the same time. They are both inextricably interlinked. This is incredibly difficult to achieve in practice, especially when internal turf wars occur.

In reality, process change tends to follow structural change. If anything, it should happen the other way around. That is, you decide what core business processes you need and then build an organisation structure around them.

MATRIX ORGANISATIONS

Most of us are well used to seeing organisation structures as functional silos. From a performance perspective, we need to understand the strengths and weaknesses of such structures intimately. Organisation designers need to have the experience to recognise when the textbook approach has been eschewed in favour of such considerations as ego, status, car grade and the fact that the ageing sales director just happens to be an old drinking buddy of the MD!

In addition, they have to be able to show organisations that there are viable, valuable alternatives. There is no law written in stone that says the finance function has to control office administration. Equally, technical services people may have a great deal to offer the sales function.

Matrix organisations are one alternative to traditional structures but they may not be the easiest to manage. The intention with a matrix organisation is to cut across hierarchical, functional and departmental boundaries and demarcation. It tries to improve organisational effectiveness by reducing barriers.

However, ask any matrix organisation to draw its organisation chart and it often looks like a traditional, hierarchical structure with just the addition of quite a few 'dotted line' relationships and reporting lines. In effect, each person still only has one 'boss' (a first principle of good organisation design?) but they can interact with other departments more easily.

Nevertheless, a good designer should know how to help the organisation structure itself to best suit the type of business operation it is in. Perhaps we can have the best of both worlds – a well defined, well structured organisation with few barriers, a culture that welcomes and encourages the cross-fertilisation of ideas and a genuine sense of teamwork and *esprit de corps*.

THE OFFICE EQUIPMENT COMPANY

In order to represent what we have just covered graphically, let us consider the example of a company marketing, selling and servicing office equipment. This is currently structured in a very conventional way (*see* Figure 14.1). The Managing Director sits at the top of the organisation with three functional silos headed by the respective directors.

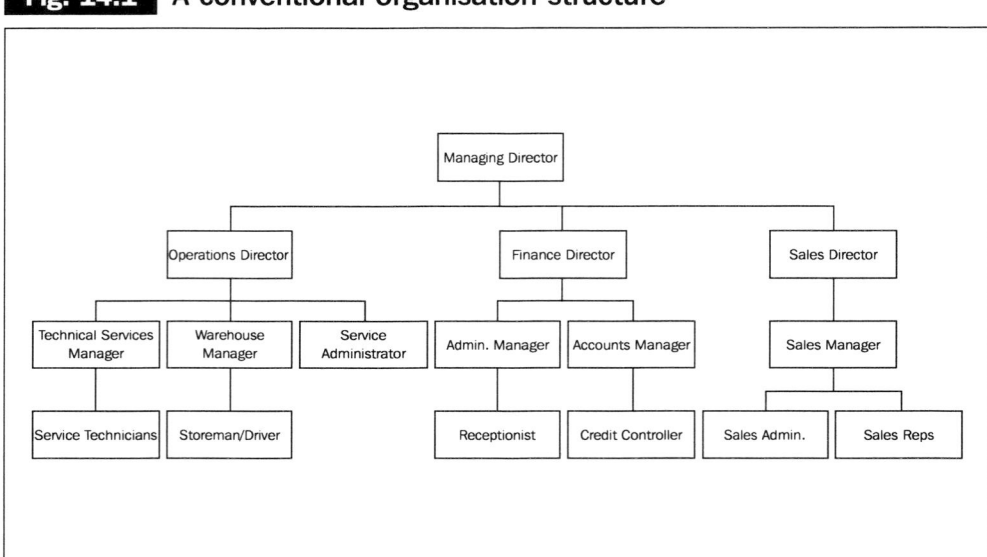

Fig. 14.1 A conventional organisation structure

As long as everyone looks after his or her own area, you might not expect anything to be wrong with this type of structure. The sales people market and sell the products; the operations and technical services people deliver and maintain the equipment. Just as in the Double-Glazing 'R' Us example given in Chapter 8, if everyone performs there are not too many problems.

Now let us look at the performance measures that might be applied to this business. Is the sales director targeted on sales volume, sales turnover, cost of sales or profit? The only really added value measure is profit, that is the value that is added to the business after all operational costs have been taken into account.

It is obvious that a high percentage of the cost of sales is likely to be outside the control of the sales director though: delivery and installation costs, any costs associated with after-sales service and even the costs of the accounts function who have to make sure the goods are paid for.

Meanwhile, the operations director could be subjected to cost and quality performance measures. If he does not manage the performance of his own team well, not only will this affect costs but it will also affect profit, of course. So why not set profit targets for both of these, if not all three directors?

In practice there would need to be at least two levels of performance measures, say a top level of profit in conjunction with a secondary level of cost and quality. This company may not be as keen on profit as market share at a particular time so these measures themselves may change.

Companies structured in this functional way rely on the cooperation and trust of each team to achieve results. This type of silo structure has served most companies well for many years. However, as competition becomes fiercer, any weaknesses in this structure soon become apparent. The sales person has to offer shorter call-out times to keep up with the rest of the market. This places enormous pressures on the technical service staff. These pressures build up and can often result in directors defending their corner rather than developing cross-functional solutions to difficult operational problems.

The worst-case scenario is when employees in one department are ordered not to cooperate with other departments without the agreement of their own boss. This happens and I can remember one occasion where a despatch manager I knew would not allow his operators to work with a production team to get a shipment out on time purely because of internal politics.

Demarcated performance measures and silo structures can breed this sort of ridiculous behaviour if not kept in check. Our greater understanding of the importance of processes should help us to overcome this type of problem. So let us look at some of the processes used by the XYZ Office Products Company.

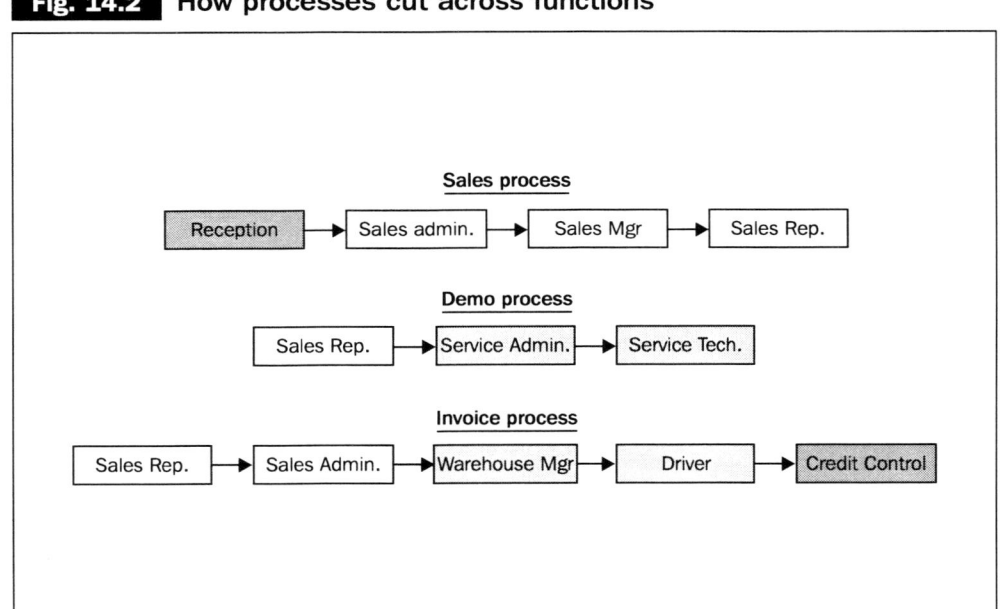

Fig. 14.2 How processes cut across functions

Sales process: Reception → Sales admin. → Sales Mgr → Sales Rep.

Demo process: Sales Rep. → Service Admin. → Service Tech.

Invoice process: Sales Rep. → Sales Admin. → Warehouse Mgr → Driver → Credit Control

In Figure 14.2 we have identified three separate processes: the sales, demonstration and invoicing processes. You might already have noticed, however, that we have drawn these slightly differently, end to end rather than on top of each other. The different boxes actually represent jobs and jobholders rather than process activities. So the sales administrator will have a range of tasks some of which will form part of the sales process (administering sales orders). They may also include other activities, such as ordering sales stationery, which could be part of an entirely different process, such as marketing.

The different shading in the boxes denotes which jobholders belong to which function. So we can see that the invoice process involves employees from all three departments. Although all of this should be fairly obvious to everyone in the company, it is made absolutely clear when illustrated in this way.

This type of diagram can be produced in a few minutes if we are trying to ensure that all departments know what their responsibilities are and encourage better cooperation. For example, imagine if we wanted to improve cashflow through the business; each of these processes has a direct impact. Any inefficiencies, say a delay in processing an order, is bound to have a negative effect on cashflow because revenue flows more slowly.

Anyone with experience of process analysis will normally start to analyse inefficient processes, in the first instance, by trying to measure the time it takes to complete any particular process cycle, such as the issuing of a proper invoice. This does not automatically mean investigating the workrate of the sales administrator; it could be that the issuing of an invoice is dependent on the time it takes the warehouse team to send a copy of the despatch form to the sales office.

If all the people in the process work together the process can be made to operate as efficiently as possible. But how about changing the process? Why cannot the receptionist produce invoices if they have some time between other duties? Well, the receptionist reports to someone outside the sales function. How happy would the sales director feel handing over this activity to another department, whether it made good commercial sense or not? This would reduce his empire and leave him with less control.

We can now see the interrelationship between process and structure. Get this right and you have a chance of improving individual, team and organisational performance. Get it wrong and everybody could be sailing against the wind.

If you have no experience of process analysis or improvement then you should be aware that there are usually five stages to go through. It is often a chicken and the egg question of where exactly you start. My suggested starting point is always looking for performance improvement targets first, then analysing which process improvements might help.

FIVE PHASES OF PERFORMANCE IMPROVEMENT THROUGH PROCESS REDESIGN

1. *Defining performance measures*

   Stretching objectives in the business plan could suggest you look at processes for improvement. A 10 per cent cost reduction target suggests that maybe some of this can be achieved through process efficiency improvement.

   Some baseline measure should be established and an improvement target set. Is the process to be made shorter, more efficient, less costly? Or is the performance issue one of improving the quality of service to the customer?

2. *Identifying processes*

   You cannot start to improve processes unless you first identify exactly which processes you want to improve. This may be stating the blindingly obvious but it is important to be reasonably precise about which processes need improving. This will inevitably involve mapping the process/es.

3. *Performance gap analysis*

   Once the process and measures are made explicit you have a basis for analysing what is causing the gap. Gap analysis is at the root of all improvement programmes. In short, is the process in question 5 per cent slower than it needs to be to achieve the desired results in the business plan?

4. *Process redesign*

   Process analysis will highlight where possible redesign will result in improvement. However, this is where process re-engineering can come unstuck. *Do not try to redesign a process without having fully considered the individuals in the existing process and those who will be involved in the newly designed process.*

   New processes mean new roles. This, in turn, has many implications in terms of capability, training, motivation, reward and performance.

5. *Implementation*

   The implementation of new processes has to be handled very carefully for the reasons identified in point 4 above. Even a small process change can have widespread repercussions.

   As much planning and advance communication as possible should help to ensure that any new processes are implemented successfully.

15

Connecting performance, knowledge management, and human and intellectual capital

- If that is the answer – what was the question again? 143
- Putting people on the balance sheet 144
- There is 'performance' and then there is *performance* 145
- Performance and innovation 146
- Knowledge management and performance 147

IF THAT IS THE ANSWER – WHAT WAS THE QUESTION AGAIN?

Anyone looking at the latest ideas being promoted on the business conference circuit could be forgiven for thinking that managing knowledge and intellectual capital is the answer to everything. I am not sure, though, whether everybody is equally agreed on what the original question or problem was.

That said, one of the most interesting and exciting developments in organisational and management theory over the last few years is the increasing interest in looking at employees as human capital and trying to maximise the use of, and return from, this capital. You may think there is nothing particularly new in this, that it is just new jargon to replace the old adage that 'our people are our greatest asset'. Not so.

It may still be very early days, but there is a fundamental shift in organisational thinking in some quarters. Its advent may well have been generated by the downsizing débâcle of the early 1990s that left a trail of depleted, weakened organisations. Downsizing definitely brought with it cost savings but many observers felt, even if they could not measure, that it had come at a price in terms of lost human potential.

There has always been a willingness, among some leaders, to adhere to the notion of people being the organisation's greatest asset. Yet, despite its inherent truth, it was always nothing more than another of the great corporate lies. There was never the means for measuring this type of capital; accountants' methods could not cope with the people asset. Double entry bookkeeping was never applied to people. The liability was always shown but never the corresponding asset value.

Even today, in a new wave of merger and takeover activity, companies such as BP and Amoco join forces partly to achieve billions of pounds in savings through greater economies of scale. Whether there are any synergies between the two businesses is debatable. But if a company can have this much effect on its bottom line, just by taking over another company, then people are still not really being seen as the greatest asset. Quite the contrary, most of the savings are coming through reducing the people asset via large-scale redundancies.

As far as the City is concerned, perhaps the BP Amoco merger is a coup both in strategic as well as cold, commercial terms. But there must be another side to the equation. Maybe some of the thousands of employees who have lost their jobs were never going to make much difference to BP Amoco. But surely these two companies have divested themselves of some assets that would have added more value. Either way, this is not catered for in the figures. It is as though you can sack thousands of employees without any consideration of what the debit side of this transaction is.

None of this detracts from the fact that the BP Amoco merger, and similar mergers, currently might make sound financial and commercial sense. The problem is more long term. The deal makers of today will no doubt still want to make big deals in years to come. The relentless pressures imposed by the need to improve shareholder value will always mean that large corporations will seek significant improvements. But in ten years' time will there be many big deals left to make in the oil industry?

There are likely to be fewer players by then and competition regulations will call a halt to further rationalisation of the industry at some stage. Also, all of the serious economies of scale will already have been absorbed, reported as savings and reflected in the share price. Where do such organisations turn then for their next step improvements? There will inevitably be a sharper focus on maximising value from human capital then but it will only happen if they start out along that road now.

PUTTING PEOPLE ON THE BALANCE SHEET

As a rugby fan, and a shareholder in my favourite club, I was sorry to see from this year's annual report that the club is, yet again, making quite a substantial loss. The balance sheet does not look too bad because the assets of the club seem to match its liabilities. Obviously, one of the biggest costs in a modern, professional rugby club is the players' salaries. These are shown quite clearly. Yet I cannot find any reference in the accounts to the actual value of these players, undoubtedly the club's greatest asset.

Surely it is not unreasonable or unrealistic to actually put a figure in the balance sheet. There are probably several ways to do this. It could be a multiple of the players' salary bill, a calculation of the total potential transfer fees or perhaps a calculation of the difference in annual gate receipts compared to the lowest club in the league.

None of these would be a perfect measure and would be open to argument, but they would start to put some figures on the real value of human capital. Also, as measurement affects behaviour, attitudes to managing people and performance would change. Even if the figures were not totally accurate, there is not much wrong with guesstimating such figures – accountants have been doing it for years and just making it look more of a science than it really is. Goodwill calculations are a very good example of this.

Any self-respecting entrepreneur will quite happily spend money on an investment, as long they believe they can achieve an acceptable return. Why is this simple logic not applied to human capital? If someone, whose total employment costs are £50,000 per annum, can generate say £60,000 worth of income or value (i.e. a net 20 per cent return on human capital) then why should they not continue to be employed. Companies who get rid of such employees are really just admitting that they do not know how to achieve a proper return from their investment in their people. Even worse, there is a very good chance that they were achieving an acceptable return on many of their employees but could not distinguish between the good and the bad. This does not seem to me to be something they should be praised for by the City.

What and how we measure really does influence attitudes and ways of thinking. If we do not measure something it is our way of saying it is not important. It has always struck me as curious, for example, why accountants only measure the cost of human resources (they do not actually refer to them as capital yet). They obviously do not see the value of people as important. This, of course, is nonsensical. They do not actually measure human capital because they do not have the means to do so. Regardless of the reasons why, the result is the same. The whole concept of human capital and how it generates value is a subject that has been ignored for far too long.

Surely, though, that is the whole point: people costs are just that, costs. There is no sense of this being an 'investment'. There is no true appraisal of the calculation of expected returns. Moreover, without this calculation, there can be no meaningful performance measures.

There have been many and various factors that have influenced thinking in this area, particularly in the last decade. So many young entrepreneurs have left their cosy, conservative corporations to set out on their own and have achieved enormous success in the growth areas of IT and communications. Obviously, large corporations look on with a sense of helplessness and envy, wondering how they can identify and then harness the potential value of such employees.

For this reason intellectual property rights have been a hot topic. This is one way in which organisations try to tap into all of this latent, burgeoning talent that they just happened to have stumbled on.

THERE IS 'PERFORMANCE' AND THEN THERE IS *PERFORMANCE*

The first two parts of this book really focused on *measuring and improving individual and team performance*. This *will always, ultimately, be a very narrow and rather limited way of improving organisational performance.*

Just as I came to understand the notion of latent demand in economics so there is an enormous amount of latent potential in our human resource which is just waiting to be tapped. Suggestion schemes are a reasonably quick indicator of how much of that potential is being tapped.

No doubt some cynics would argue that some of the old-style suggestion schemes only generated abusive suggestions from some of the more recalcitrant employees. Good ideas, though, are there just waiting to be unearthed. The simplest way to measure suggestion schemes is to measure the number of (acceptable) suggestions per employee. So 100 suggestions in a year, from a workforce of 100 employees results in a 100 per cent suggestion rate. This, of course, does not mean that every employee makes a suggestion. In some Japanese companies, though, the suggestion scheme rate is as high as 500 per cent. Many of these will be converted into cost reductions, quality improvements or even new product innovations. *But only if, strategically, the culture, systems and processes have been created to enable this to happen.*

One company that seems to achieve the most added value, from the majority of its employees is Toyota. They may not be everybody's employer of choice but for those who work there they know what the contract is. It is made very explicit. Employees are expected to come to work and bring their brains with them. The company does everything it can to generate improvement ideas and it has been doing so for many years. So how much value has this added?

In a league table of the top 10 automotive companies produced by Reuters in May 1998, Toyota was number one in terms of shareholder value with a market capitalisation of $98.61 billion. Ford came fourth with a figure of $51.80 billion.

While these figures are, in themselves, very revealing, they are even more incredible when you realise that Ford had a sales turnover of $153.63 billion against Toyota's $69.22 billion. In other words, Toyota is half the size of Ford in sales terms, but worth twice as much in the market. They are performing four times better than Ford by this definition. They must be managing their employees to maximise value very successfully.

PERFORMANCE AND INNOVATION

Even the hardest, most cynical businessperson would have to agree that there is potential to be tapped, but how do you go about it? Not by running creativity and innovation courses. Look at this quote from an *Economist* survey.

Two things set apart all organisations with a record of innovation. One is that they foster individuals who are internally driven ... The second is that they do not leave innovation to chance: they pursue it systematically. They actively search for change (the root of all innovation), then carefully evaluate its potential for an economic or social return.

Invariably, breakthrough innovations require a fundamental rethink. Sometimes they come from dusting off ideas that failed to make it in the past.

(*The Economist* – Innovation in Industry Survey, February 1999)

I think this quote says it all. Very little happens by chance. Employee performance and innovation make good bedfellows. I also agree that innovative breakthroughs come from 'dusting off' old ideas. That is exactly what this book is trying to do.

KNOWLEDGE MANAGEMENT AND PERFORMANCE

I mentioned earlier that I had never come across an organisation that did not believe it had a communications problem. If ever proof of this were needed then the advent of 'knowledge management' provides it. There may not be any precise, agreed definition of what knowledge management is, but in essence it is a conscious effort to capture and share the organisation's expertise. Surely the fact that this is seen as something new and now has to be 'managed' indicates that the organisations pursuing it have not been very good at it in the past.

Put even more bluntly, if an organisation has a 'knowledge manager', then it is not a learning organisation. It is having to make a great effort to ensure that it uses the knowledge and expertise of its employees to greatest effect. A high-performing organisation will, to a great extent, do this automatically.

Of course, the growth in computer systems and, more recently, the Internet and intranets have led some to the conclusion that knowledge management is, primarily, a function of IT systems. These are the same people who promised us the paperless office many years ago (can you remember that far back?) and who thrive on data (not information) production.

Interestingly, the knowledge management proponents did not choose to call it information management. I can only presume that is because information management proved to be such a misnomer when it was used originally. Surely what we want is applied knowledge, not knowledge *per se* (remember that knowledge is only level 2 in terms of understanding.) It is amazing how new terminology can appear, paradoxically, to be taking a step backwards.

As an HR practitioner, my view is that if knowledge management is a worthwhile activity then there are many other conditions that will have to exist if its potential is to be maximised. There needs to be a sharing culture, the structure of the organisation needs to be open to the cross-fertilisation of ideas, and systems need to be put into place to capture useful knowledge (the last thing any organisation wants is knowledge for the sake of it).

Certainly, applied knowledge requires agreement and successful implementation before it can be said to be adding value. Moreover, the story of the supply manager at the oil company in Chapter 12 shows, very clearly, how human nature does not automatically lend itself to the sharing of knowledge.

This is not a book about knowledge management but any prospective high-performing organisation needs to be well aware of the need for maximising the know-how and intellectual capital of its employees. This does not mean it has to create a knowledge management team but it has to be constantly aware of the organisational barriers that exist which reduce the opportunities that this latent know-how represents.

If you believe you work in an organisation that is good at managing human capital, intellectual capital and knowledge then it might be a good idea to look at Tool 13 (*see* appendix). Draw up a set of simple questions to gauge what level of understanding exists on these concepts, at senior and middle management level. You should be aiming for level 5 at least.

16

The role of human resource management in performance measurement and management

- HR strategy and performance   151
- Why traditional appraisal schemes don't work   152
- The advent of performance management systems   153
- Why the personnel function needs to change   154
- The HR function as performance management function   155
- The need for a specialist performance measurement and management unit   155
- Training in performance measurement   156

HR STRATEGY AND PERFORMANCE

Throughout the book we have constructed a framework with many different elements. The only remaining element to put in place is an HR strategy that is entirely focused on performance. There are actually two questions we need to ask HR directors:

- Do you have an HR strategy?
- What is it focused on?

Although most HR directors would tell you that they have a strategy, it is more likely that they have a series of personnel policies, many of which are nothing to do with performance. They may have an equal opportunities policy because the law says they should. They have a training policy because they believe in training, not because they can show it impacts on performance. I would not regard this as an HR strategy.

An HR strategy is not about 'business as usual'. The only reason for having an HR strategy is to bring about organisational change. Anything else is just a collection of policy statements. A good HR strategy is directly linked to strategic business objectives. It sets out the most appropriate organisation structures and processes. Only then can it be used as a basis for developing HR policies and procedures.

We can see the difference effective HR strategies can make but you need to know what to look for. When have you been to a hotel where the service is indifferent? I once arrived at a central London hotel, with only minutes to spare, before having to deliver a presentation at a conference. Looking flustered and out of breath I asked the man behind the cloakroom counter where the conference room was. He immediately leapt out from behind the counter and said 'follow me, sir'. He then led me to the other end of this large hotel and left me at the door to the conference room with literally only seconds left. I was extremely grateful to him.

This could have happened in any decent hotel, except that this particular hotel chain expects this standard from all of its employees. They are selected to possess these qualities. They are trained to react in this way, when this sort of situation arises. This man's supervisor would not blow a gasket if he found his post unmanned. That is the way this hotel group operates. They go to great lengths and great expense to make sure it works like this. They do it because their business strategy is founded on the belief that this will help them beat their competitors. They won the 'Business Hotel of the Year Award' that year.

You may want to try and learn something from an organisation such as this. Most organisations will indulge in a bit of benchmarking, either on an informal or formal basis. Obviously there is a great deal we can learn from both competitors and other organisations in different industries but with similar problems.

However, like all techniques, it is only as good as the use you make of it. Use it with intelligence and it will help. Just copy what other people are doing and it will not help. If you look at just one aspect (e.g. how this man was trained) then you miss the even more important point that this man felt empowered to leave his post. You also miss the fact that his supervisor would reinforce this behaviour. All parts of the strategy have to fit together for it to work.

Personnel and HR practitioners are notorious for seeking out 'best practice' or just copying blue-chip organisations, without asking serious questions of the real benefits from such approaches. As a consequence it is a profession replete with fads, flavours of the month and the weird and wonderful. The use of management competencies, 360° feedback systems and the setting up of corporate universities have all generated enormous amounts of activity without any clear evidence of whether they lead to improved individual or organisational performance.

What we are trying to find out, when observing other organisations, are the things they do which help them to get the best performance out of their people. This is certainly not a straightforward exercise. What is it, for example, that helps Toyota to achieve such a high performance and such a high value as a business? Is it their lean production process, their life-time employment policy, their total quality methodology? It is all of these things and all of these things are possible because it has an HR strategy directly linked to business strategy founded on some simple principles that work. It also took them many years to reap all of the benefits.

WHY TRADITIONAL APPRAISAL SCHEMES DON'T WORK

Perhaps the bluntest instrument in the personnel department's armoury has always been the traditional appraisal scheme. The one-to-one discussions between supervisor and subordinate have become a very tired old idea. Also, what looks a nice idea on paper is often regarded as a real chore.

One relatively recent development in this area is the idea of peer reviews or some sort of assessment by those who work with, or around, the employee in question rather than *for* them. The most well known 'product' is 360° feedback. I say 'product' because it is virtually impossible to administer a 360° appraisal scheme unless you buy the software to demonstrate the various attributes or competencies that are being addressed (a consultant's dream).

We could have a very lengthy debate about appraisal schemes and the extent to which they are part of an effective EPMMS. *My own simple view about appraisal is that good managers don't need it and bad employees don't want it.*

So who does it serve? If you are self-motivated, and your boss takes a natural interest in your performance and personal development, then formal appraisal schemes have very little to offer. A blank sheet of paper will suffice.

If you are a poor performer, or your boss is not comfortable with anything other than a very limited focus on the task in hand, then appraisal discussions can just become an awkward meeting. This then degenerates into platitudes and the necessary filling in of forms until the next year.

THE ADVENT OF PERFORMANCE MANAGEMENT SYSTEMS

Formal 'performance management systems', as an idea, have been around for a long time. However, for the most part, it was just the personnel department's usual appraisal system with new stationery. As we have seen above, though, old style appraisal systems never really delivered the goods. Early attempts to improve this situation did not fare much better. This was as much to do with unclear objectives as it was a lack of good performance measures.

Here is an example of just such muddled thinking, taken from *Personnel Management* in November 1992. This is from an article about Zeneca Pharmaceutical's 'new' performance management system. The designers of the system were asked how they would know if the new system was working or not. This was the reply:

> *As far as progress towards our ultimate aim of performance management is concerned pre-tax profit growth may not be the most appropriate measure of success; the indicators may be more non-specific and subjective but in business culture terms just as meaningful.*

This quote begs many more questions than it answers. Probably the worst offence is to have a performance management system (*sic*) that does not regard pre-tax profit growth as a criterion for success. More obscurely, what are these other 'non-specific indicators' and what does the phrase 'business culture terms' mean?

Basically there are two conclusions that the reader can come to. Either Zeneca have discovered something that no other organisation has and is genuinely ahead of the game in performance management. Alternatively, to the more sceptical eye, this is 100 per cent pure bullshit.

I raised this issue at an HRM conference in 1996, where I was speaking on the subject of performance measurement. The theme of my presentation was how to link soft and hard measures and I used this quotation on one of my slides. As I knew it might offend Zeneca, I checked the delegate list, in advance, to see whether any Zeneca representatives were present, only to find that they had sent not just one but two delegates (perhaps they have a communication problem at Zeneca).

My presentation was the first session after lunch. At the precise moment, when I was just about to put this particular slide up, in walked two delegates who had returned late. To avoid any great disturbance they sat down right in the front row, about six feet from where I was speaking, just close enough for me to pick out the word Zeneca on their name badges.

For a split second, I considered pulling this particular slide but then thought what the hell and decided to go ahead with it. Only this time, I mentioned to the audience that we had some delegates from Zeneca in the audience and I wondered how they might respond to my criticism. To this challenge, one of the Zeneca delegates responded, with a wry smile, and just said quietly, 'oh, we have moved onto something else since then.'

WHY THE PERSONNEL FUNCTION NEEDS TO CHANGE

As an HRM professional myself, I could hardly write this manual without reference to the wider implications for HRM in performance measurement and management. It is amazing that anyone could try to write anything useful on the subject of performance measurement without concentrating on the human angle, and yet to date that is what they seem to do. Hence the lack of books on performance measurement with the specific word employee or people in the title.

At the international conference on 'Performance Measurement – Theory and Practice' held at Cambridge University in 1998 (interestingly the first to be held there) there was a distinct lack of speakers who came to the subject from the human angle.

Some of the speakers appeared to assume that the only real issue in performance measurement was the ability to *measure* performance. This book has tried to demonstrate that what is equally important, if not more important, are very human issues such as management attitudes, motivation, fear, encouragement and reward.

The drier academics seem to think that producing the 'right' performance measures is the key to organisational performance, as though just having the measures means you will achieve the targets set. Any practising manager would quickly dispel this notion. If it were that easy who would need managers? Equally, if most managers were already good at measuring and managing performance we would not be discussing the subject here.

At the time of writing, the personnel profession (not the HR profession) is facing some of its toughest challenges ever. A great deal of personnel work is transactional, administrative and often unnecessarily bureaucratic. It is viewed as a necessary evil by most organisations and one that should come at a minimum cost. Consequently, there is a great deal of interest in outsourcing as much personnel work as possible to reduce costs. This has been happening in the USA for some considerable time but it is now starting to rear its head on a global basis.

I am a great critic of modern HR fads but it is because I firmly believe that *the HR function should be the employee performance function*. If those who work in the function want to stay employed they would do well to become the company's performance experts.

THE HR FUNCTION AS PERFORMANCE MANAGEMENT FUNCTION

I have worked in HRM for many years, and when I started to specialise in employee performance measurement it soon dawned on me that all HR work is really about performance measurement, management and improvement. Broadly speaking, HR's aim is to find, attract, select, recruit, train, motivate and reward the best employees it can lay its hands on. It wants to find good performers, ensure they fit in well and perform for their organisation, develop their potential performance to the full and then reward them accordingly so that they do not lose that highly valuable asset. Every HR activity can be regarded as a performance management activity.

Although this should always have been the case, in reality most personnel practitioners would have looked at you as though you had landed from Mars if you suggested to them that, really, they worked in a performance management function. This is why many organisations do not want them any more. The HR practitioners of the future will be performance management specialists and experts if they are to survive at all.

THE NEED FOR A SPECIALIST PERFORMANCE MEASUREMENT AND MANAGEMENT UNIT

Performance measurement is big enough, and potentially of high enough value, to warrant a trained, specialist team.

I have also tried to emphasise that a strategic approach must be adopted to the subject of EPMMS. Part of this strategic approach should be a human resource management strategy. Interestingly, NatWest Bank's HR function had a 'vision' statement back in 1993 that said it wanted to be:

> *... a world class Human Resource function which is first choice for the Business, Staff and Customers.*

Apart from the fact that this does not make much sense (how will customers ever meet the HR function?) NatWest is currently fighting off a number of predators because of its failure to perform. So much for strategies based on balanced business scorecards that include employee measures.

TRAINING IN PERFORMANCE MEASUREMENT

Whoever is tasked with setting up an EPMMS there is an enormous amount of training and education that will have to take place, and this is assuming that an effective HR strategy is already in place. Anyone working in this area has to have a high level of understanding (level 6?) of organisation culture, organisation design, processes, measurement systems, data analysis, performance appraisal, objective setting, human relations and a whole host of other skills and techniques. This manual may not have all the answers or be able to provide all of the training needed but it will hopefully provide some clear guidelines to get them started.

Appendix

Employee performance measurement and management tools

- Tool 1: Where are you in employee performance measurement – a primer 159
- Tool 2: Producing an employee performance distribution curve 160
- Tool 3: Using the distribution curve to improve performance 161
- Tool 4: Establishing what factors contribute to improved individual performance 163
- Tool 5: Does motivation influence performance? 164
- Tool 6: Creating a closed loop feedback system 167
- Tool 7: How to set performance objectives 169
- Tool 8: Personal added value and performance review (PAVPR) 172
- Tool 9: Which of your activities add the most value? 174
- Tool 10: Spot the performance and added value measures 176
- Tool 11: Performance trend chart 177
- Tool 12: Redesigning the organisation to improve performance 178
- Tool 13: Checking levels of understanding 181

Appendix

TOOL 1: WHERE ARE YOU IN EMPLOYEE PERFORMANCE MEASUREMENT – A PRIMER

As with any teach yourself manual the best place – in fact the only place – to start from is where you are. So try answering the following questions, then consider what actions you should take first.

1. You need employee measures. What 'measures' do you currently use?
   - Operational data (sales, output, customer service levels, productivity)?
   - Do you try to gauge individual competence in the job?
   - Do you have some data to produce a performance distribution curve?

2. You need a performance review system. Do you have one?
   - Is there some standard paperwork?
   - Is it just based on superior/subordinate appraisal?

3. Do you manage underperformance?
   - Has anyone been fired for persistent underperformance?
   - Do you currently have anyone working on targets to bring them up to an acceptable level?
   - Are time limits set for improvement?
   - Do underperformers receive less pay or other benefits?

4. What about performance related pay?
   - Do you have it?
   - Does it work, i.e. does it reward the right people for the right performance?
   - Are bonuses awarded purely on overall company performance?

5. How good are you at retaining staff?
   - Do you know what your staff turnover is?
   - What about stability?
   - Do you have a target for both?
   - Are your management accounts founded on achieving this level?

6. What level of understanding do you have about performance measures?
   - Do you know the difference between an activity measure and a process measure?
   - What constitutes an added value performance measure?
   - What is the difference between someone performing and someone adding value?

Appendix

TOOL 2: PRODUCING AN EMPLOYEE PERFORMANCE DISTRIBUTION CURVE

The easiest and simplest way to produce the performance curve discussed in Chapter 3 is to sit down with a manager or group of managers and take them through these simple steps. Alternatively, practise first by doing the exercise alone for the employees under your personal control.

1. The objective is to achieve improved company performance through measurable improvements in individual performance. The technique to be used is very easy to understand and should make each manager's job easier.

2. In the event of any strong objections put their minds at rest and reassure them that this exercise is purely introductory. Also, for confidentiality, no one will be allowed to see the results of the exercise, outside of this group, without the manager's express permission.

3. Explain that measurement is an absolutely key principle and so you are asking them to place a performance measure on each of their employees.

4. Explain the measuring scale is from 1 to 10 with 10 being the maximum/best score. Each employee has to be scored and this 'performance' measure is all-embracing. In other words, if two employees are equal in every respect but one is a worse timekeeper then that employee may have a slightly lower score.

5. Offer further guidelines from the sample chart by indicating that any score of 3 or less indicates that this employee is not performing at the minimum level acceptable. Equally, anyone with a score of 8 or more can be regarded as a superior performer. Everyone between 3 and 8 is acceptable or satisfactory.

6. Ask them to now score each member of their team/department. Using the type of form shown below they can do this very simply.

Employee ID (can be anonymous)	*Performance score*
A	5
B	5
C	7
D	6
E	9
F	2
G	5
H	4
I	4
J	6

TOOL 3: USING THE DISTRIBUTION CURVE TO IMPROVE PERFORMANCE

To complete this exercise you should have already completed Tool 2. Ideally, you will have collected performance scores for a minimum of 30 employees so that there is a greater possibility of producing a normal distribution curve. However, any number of performance scores can be used. Add up the number of employees in each performance category (e.g. three employees are given a score of 4) and plot it on the chart.

The chart below shows the total number of employees for each performance score.

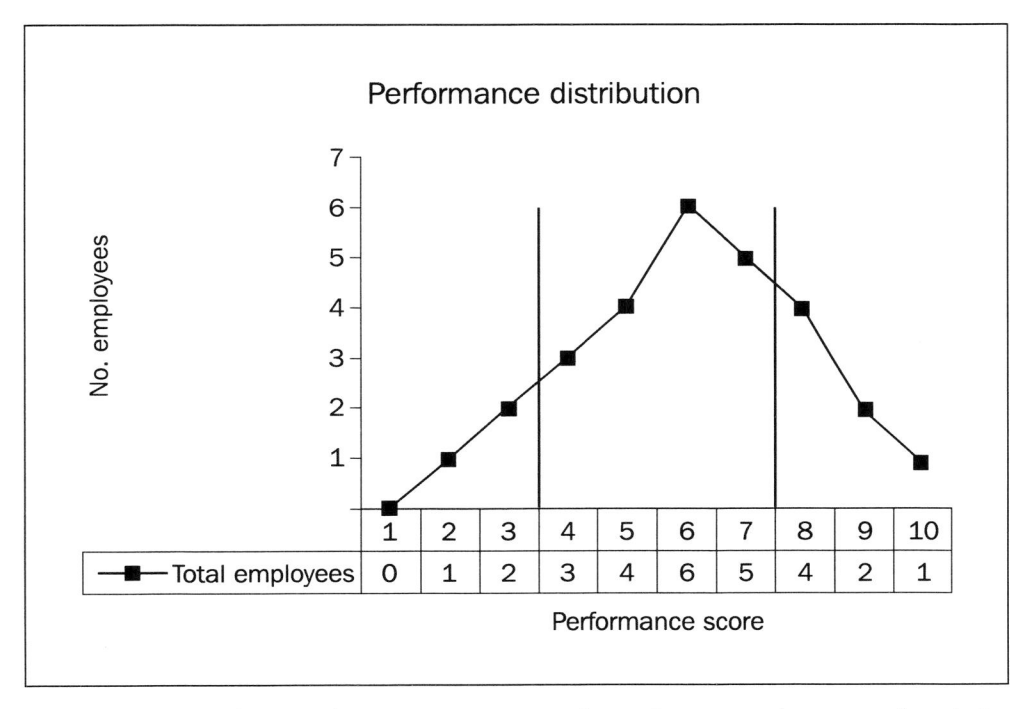

Performance distribution

Performance score	1	2	3	4	5	6	7	8	9	10
Total employees	0	1	2	3	4	6	5	4	2	1

Produce a similar graph using your own data. Once you have produced the graph follow these steps.

1. *Managing underperformance*

   Look at where the graph starts. Anyone below the first cut-off line (i.e. 3 or less) is unacceptable. This should immediately prompt a discussion along the following lines:
   - Why are these employees below this line?
   - If they have only recently been employed how long are they allowed before they have to be up to the minimum standard?
   - If they are established employees why is their current performance unacceptable?

- Have they been told it is unacceptable? Would they accept this judgement?
- What solutions might there be in this section of the curve?

2. *Improving average performance*

    A different perspective is required for the middle section of the curve. These employees are already acceptable and so need to be motivated to perform better. Again, there will be many ways to improve performance.

3. *Managing superior performers*

    At the highest end of the distribution curve are those employees who are already highly motivated and performing very well. Discussing performance improvement with such staff is a totally different proposition. How might such a discussion be structured?

4. Try producing the same sort of curve by looking at just one aspect of performance such as productivity. What actions would this particular curve prompt?

5. Finally, how will the cut-off points change over the next year? Will those at performance level 4 be acceptable next year?

TOOL 4: ESTABLISHING WHAT FACTORS CONTRIBUTE TO IMPROVED INDIVIDUAL PERFORMANCE

In Chapter 11 we explored some of the key elements which contribute to individual performance. This tool is designed to take this a stage further and should be used as part of a constructive and positive performance discussion.

The objective of this exercise is to choose one particular person in one particular role or position (at any level) in your team and consider how the performance of this individual, in this role, can be maximised.

First consider all of the following factors (and any others you can think of) in relation to how they influence performance:

- Physical ability
- Educational attainment, intelligence level
- Expertise, specialist knowledge
- Experience for this role
- Personal motivation, productivity, effort and willingness
- Authority level
- Relationships with own team
- Relationships outside the team
- Communication
- Domestic situation

Each heading can point to a possible cause of this employee not performing as well as they could.

Once some potential causes have been established you can consider which factors this employee has some control over and which they do not.

Now, what options do you have to improve their contribution or performance? Do you need to speak to someone else? Is there just a gap in knowledge or training that can be filled? Are there any areas where the employee just does not possess the necessary capability?

What else impinges or impacts on their effectiveness?

TOOL 5: DOES MOTIVATION INFLUENCE PERFORMANCE?

This is an exercise to identify what really motivates you and improves your effectiveness.

The conventional wisdom suggests that, above everything else, we must motivate our employees if we are to expect them to perform. It sounds an eminently sensible idea but what *exactly* does that mean? If we adopt just a simple, analytical approach to this question and ask some basic questions, what conclusions do we come to? For example, consider the following questions in relation to your own views on motivation and effectiveness:

1. What specifically influences your motivation (e.g. money, recognition, communication, etc.)? What provides you with real, personal satisfaction?

2. What specifically influences your effectiveness (e.g. motivation, capability, training, resources, etc.)? Alternatively, what gets in the way of your personal effectiveness?

3. Can you discern any direct link between your motivation and your personal effectiveness? Did the bonus you receive, for example, really have an impact on your effectiveness, either before or after the bonus was paid?

   Conversely, even at your lowest point in motivational terms (maybe you failed to get that promotion you wanted), did you still carry out your job effectively?

4. How much does your motivation vary over time? Are you reasonably well motivated to do a good job every working day? Do you have large swings in your levels of motivation?

5. If your motivation level can be influenced by other considerations (as in 1 above) is the effect significant and how long does it last?

6. How many types of motivator are there and are they all positive?
   - self-interest?
   - recognition?
   - altruism?
   - fear/worry/guilt?
   - business focus?
   - frustration?
   - any others?

7. Are you more motivated or less motivated by insecurity? What happens to this motivator if you are guaranteed a job for life or your job is under threat?

8. Is there a maximum and a minimum level of motivation? (And what happens when you are at the minimum/maximum?)

Appendix

We all know this whole area is complex so to make it more meaningful why not try the following exercise?

Plotting your levels of motivation and effectiveness

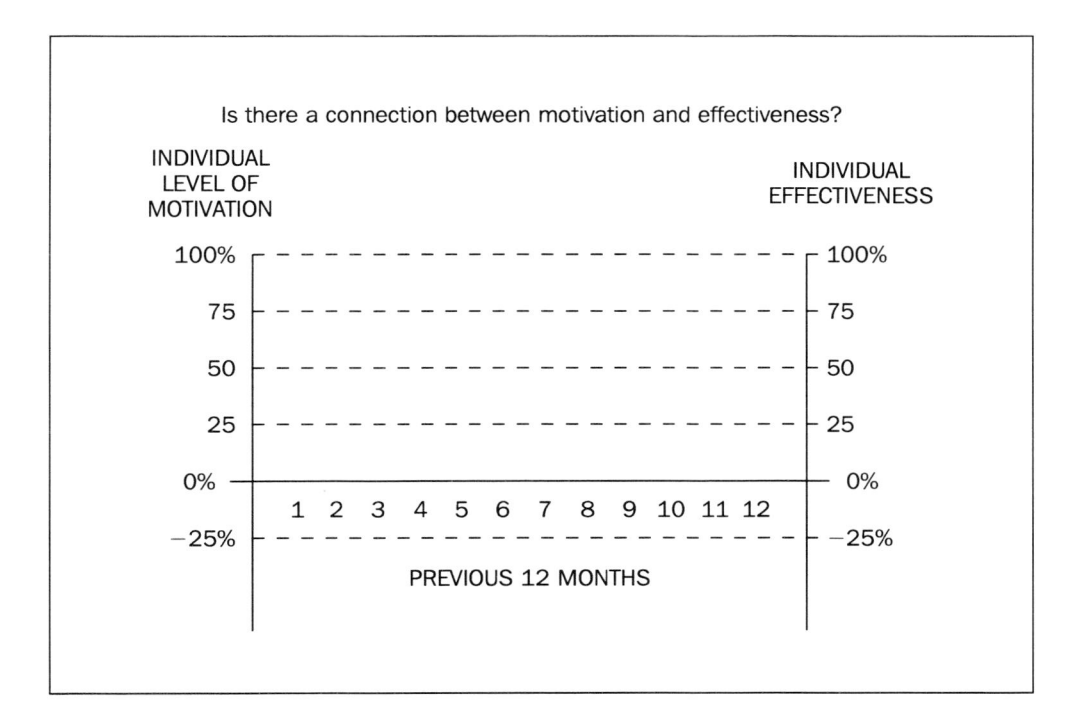

Is there a connection between motivation and effectiveness?

INDIVIDUAL LEVEL OF MOTIVATION — INDIVIDUAL EFFECTIVENESS

(Graph with vertical axes from -25% to 100% on both sides, horizontal axis showing months 1–12, labelled "PREVIOUS 12 MONTHS")

1. Complete the graph for how you believe your level of motivation has changed over the course of the year to date. (One hundred per cent would be when you were motivated to make a supreme and extraordinary effort, zero is when you feel no motivation and a minus figure would be when you actually feel de-motivated.)

2. Now complete the graph for how you believe your level of personal effectiveness (i.e. how well you did your job) has altered over the same period. Again 100 per cent is perfection, zero is totally ineffective and a negative means you actually have an adverse effect on the organisation (e.g. criticising the company in front of customers).

3. Now replot both charts to show how they would look if a range of extra motivating factors came into play, for example better rewards, a personal development programme, improved communications from the company.

4. Has either graph shifted significantly? Have you learned anything about the connection, if any, between your own pattern of motivation and your actual performance (effectiveness)? Or is your personal effort and performance level much more of a constant than you had ever previously thought?

Appendix

This Tool will probably raise as many questions as answers but the messages are quite clear. Patterns of motivation are unique to each individual. If we are to improve performance through efforts to improve motivation there are many motivating factors that must be taken into consideration, and not all of them are positive.

If we are unsure or vague about what motivates someone then the performance improvement efforts will be unfocused, poorly conceived and may have no effect on the more important issues of personal effectiveness and/or organisational performance.

If nothing else, this Tool provides a very useful framework for discussing the problematic areas of motivation and personal effectiveness with staff.

TOOL 6: CREATING A CLOSED LOOP FEEDBACK SYSTEM

If you have already read Chapter 2 you will have been introduced to the simple *Plan–Do–Check–Act* (PDCA) cycle. This is the foundation stone for continuously improving what we do. Its origins can be traced back to the plan, do, study, act 'new' way proposed by Shewart in 1929. Companies like Toyota train their staff in how to use the PDCA cycle and it is used every day. So it works.

A key part of this cycle is the element of being able to *check* that what we *do* actually had the desired effect. This necessitates having a *feedback system* that tells us whether things are improving or not. Also, it has to *close the loop* – that is, it ensures action is taken if necessary.

For example, on a training course, if we did not check who attended we would never know who has actually had what training. A simple participant registration list will enable us to check who sat in on which session. This closes the loop so that no one is asked to attend the same course twice and it picks up those nominees who have not yet attended.

We all use informal closed loops every day of our lives. The petrol gauge tells us we are running low on fuel so we top the tank up. We check our bank statement to make sure we have enough money to pay the bills. We ask friends to RSVP when we send out a party invitation.

There is nothing difficult about the concept of the PDCA cycle. However, it is intended to be a continuous loop. So if you had a *plan* to reduce costs and then checked that your costs have reduced by 10 per cent you should now embark on a new plan to reduce them further.

Your task

1. Think of the work you and your team/department do. To what extent are closed loops in place? Could you write down at least three examples of a closed loop being used?

2. If you have not consciously used a PDCA cycle before choose a performance objective, with a clear measure, and *plan* how you are going to achieve it. It does not matter at this stage how significant this improvement target is. It is more important to just try out the PDCA cycle.

    If possible ask each member of your team to produce a simple plan to improve a particular measure. It can be something extremely simple, such as a reduction in the number of errors made.

3. The PDCA cycle will, automatically, beg the question how are we measuring this problem now? So with errors, if there is no system to measure the number of errors made then a simple system will have to be set up. Normally, this would involve producing a tally chart:

Appendix

	Type of error	Tally
1	Wrong details on cover note	IIIII IIIII
2	Cover note sent out unsigned	III
3	No premium shown	II
4	Incorrect premium	I
5	Spelling error	I
	Total	12

4. Regardless of how the data is collected this has to be the starting point for the use of a PDCA cycle. Once the data has been collected an improvement target can be set. In this case the incidence of error item 1 is to be reduced by 50 per cent. Step 1 of the PDCA cycle is now complete.

5. Working through this simple example you should now ensure that you consciously stop at each stage of *do*, *check* and *act*. What you actually *do* to reduce the number of type 1 errors is now the question. Hopefully, you will choose the correct course of action (in this case there may be one employee causing most of these errors so the *do* part of the cycle is to address this with the employee concerned).

6. Although it obviously helps to get the solution 'right first time' do not worry too much at this stage. The beauty of the PDCA cycle is that it forces you to *check* whether you got it right. The *check* stage is a key element of this cycle and you can only *check* by referring back to your original measure of type-1 error rates.

7. Let us assume the worst. If the *do* action has not had the desired effect on error rates then we must move on to the *act* stage. This basically asks the question: where do you go from here? If errors have not fallen then you must think again and maybe try something else (perhaps the cause of the errors was the underwriter, not the person completing the cover note).

    The *plan* will remain the same but you now try a different *do* action, that is the underwriter needs to understand how they are causing errors to be repeated on the cover note.

8. Now we enter into the second cycle of this tool and follow exactly the same steps.

This tool is so powerful in performance measurement, management and learning that it should be taught in every organisation as part of basic training. Use the simple grid below.

Plan	Reduce type 1 errors by 50% to 5
Do	Monitor cover note writer
Check	Re-measure type 1 errors
Act	Speak to underwriter

TOOL 7: HOW TO SET PERFORMANCE OBJECTIVES

Setting objectives has always been a key part of any attempt to measure and manage performance. The idea of SMART (Specific, Measurable, Agreed, Realistic and Timebound) objectives has been around for many years but very rarely do performance objectives fully satisfy these criteria.

This tool adds a few more criteria to ensure that performance objectives drive performance improvement. They state that performance objectives should also be:

Added value objectives

Linked to measures in the business plan

Enabled in the sense that they can be achieved by the person concerned

Challenging and therefore worthwhile and motivating.

As you have probably noticed, this means all future objectives should satisfy the SMART ALEC criteria.

This Tool has been developed for several reasons:

- to clearly establish the principles of setting performance objectives;
- to provide experience of holding a performance improvement meeting/discussion;
- to act as a template for future performance meetings.

The exercise is split into four parts and ideally should be tried out in a small sample group. Work through each part of the exercise in turn.

Part 1

Imagine that you have received a message from your boss that all company car drivers are being asked to improve their petrol consumption in an effort to reduce overall car fleet costs. This is now one of your performance objectives.

You are planning to call a short meeting of company car drivers but first consider how you would address this performance question with your staff. How would you structure the meeting? How will you introduce the subject? What information would you need to have available beforehand? What objections might you anticipate?

When you have considered all of these points move on to Part 2.

Part 2

Below is a list of questions that should help to prepare for this meeting. You can use it as a template but feel free to amend or change it as you see fit.

Appendix

1. What is the specific objective and what is the timescale involved?

   Did your boss set a clear objective originally? Is it really a reduction in petrol consumption that is required or is the real objective a reduction in fuel costs? These look very similar but in fact are very different performance objectives. The start of performance measurement is having a crystal-clear objective with a specific measure.

2. What is the baseline? (And what units do you use?)

   Before you can move forward you must establish the baseline measure. Depending on the actual objective you choose the units of measure will be different. So, if it is petrol consumption it could be miles per gallon (mpg), miles per litre or even litres per mile. On the other hand fuel costs could be pence per mile.

   Once you establish the units or metrics to be used you can ask questions about current or baseline performance. So what is everyone achieving currently?

3. What is the improvement target? (And what units do you use?)

   Let us assume at this stage that the real objective is fuel cost and that the average fuel cost is 10 pence per mile. The improvement target could be set at a 10 per cent improvement, which would make the performance measure a 1 pence per mile reduction. Again, this is a very different objective to setting a mpg increase, which could be moving from 30 mpg to 33 mpg.

4. What cost constraints are there?

   You must consider cost constraints in advance of performance discussions. What if one of the team suggests that a fuel saving could be achieved by tuning all the engines more frequently? This could outweigh a 10 per cent saving on the cost per mile.

5. What other constraints are there?

   Is one given or parameter that there will be no change in the company car policy? That is, no one can change cars to achieve a higher mpg?

6. What can this individual do to help achieve this objective?

   Having set a group performance measure, have you already asked each individual about their own personal petrol consumption? The ways in which each individual can achieve their own performance objective will vary according to their existing personal performance. The worst drivers could perhaps just slow down. The best may have to just make sure they buy their petrol at the lowest price available. Interestingly, if the objective agreed was to improve mpg then buying cheaper petrol has no effect on this measure and yet it would save the company money.

7. Who else needs to be involved?

   Would you ask the fleet manager to attend the meeting? How about someone from accounts to agree how the information is to be collated and reported back?

8. What other ideas do you have which are currently outside of the constraints?

   Would everyone agree to drive diesel? Could the car policy change to allow smaller, faster cars but with better petrol consumption?

Part 3

Before moving on to Part 4 consider what principles have been established during Part 2. In other words, what have you learned from Part 2 which you will be able to use again in any performance discussion?

If you have actually tried this Tool out you will, by now, have realised that even something as straightforward as improving petrol consumption can become very complicated if you do not have well defined objectives and measures at the beginning.

Also, do people know how they are performing and do they have a yardstick to gauge their performance?

You will also appreciate that performance discussions can become quite animated (if not heated). Looking at 'averages' may mean that the best performers will be annoyed that they are being asked to improve.

There are numerous ways in which performance can be improved. Some are preferable to others.

Part 4

Now use the principles you have learned again, but start with a different performance objective for an individual employee or group of employees.

Also, consider what would be a realistic, achievable performance target.

Finally, have you considered any incentive during this exercise and, if so, what type of incentive could you use? It does not have to be financial.

TOOL 8: PERSONAL ADDED VALUE AND PERFORMANCE REVIEW (PAVPR)

This Tool is simply a set of questions that you can use to hold a performance discussion with your staff. If you already have some in-house forms for this purpose then these can act as supplementary questions or, better still, provide them with this checklist of questions to consider before you meet.

1. Which of your current activities fit into the following categories:

    Basic/operational/critical/support?

    Filling forms in is a basic operational requirement for most jobs. However, while some forms are there to support administration others are of critical importance. Consider, for instance, how important the proper completion of a surgical operation consent form is in a hospital.

    Added value?

    These are the activities that really make a difference. They can often be activities that require extra effort or new skills. So working on a cost reduction or efficiency project will be added value. Added value activities can be subject to ROI calculations

    Non-added value?

    This is an opportunity to discuss any work that seems to be superfluous. The work may be important but this employee does not realise why it is. Alternatively it could genuinely be a waste of time and effort.

2. Which of the above activities should:

    Cease?

    Any activity that has no operational requirement or is non-added value should be targeted for cessation as soon as possible.

    Be improved?

    Are there any areas for improvement which have not already been identified?

    Be undertaken elsewhere?

    Which activities would fit better with another colleague/team/department?

3. What measures of performance are already in place?

    Are performance measures already in place from the budget, operational or business plan? Does this employee own these measures, or do they not have any influence on these measures? Can they suggest any other measures that are more meaningful? Can a baseline measure and target be agreed?

4. Which activities are determined solely and exclusively by you?

   It could be that very few activities are solely the responsibility of this employee but, where they are, these should be highlighted and measures agreed.

   This question is specifically designed to discuss areas where collaboration or cooperation with another team or function will be necessary.

5. Which activities are performed in conjunction with:

   Here, following on from 4 above, performance issues have to be addressed to take into account:

   –other members of this department

   –other departments.

6. Which processes are these activities linked to? Have these processes been formally identified and mapped?

   If process maps already exist then these can be referred to. If not, then drawing a simple flow diagram can help focus on the priorities and opportunities for improvement.

7. In what ways could the processes themselves be improved?

   There should be no attempt to deal with this question unless question 6 has already been completed. Also, this will often involve other functions and this should be covered under questions 4 and 5.

8. What barriers do you perceive to such improvements?

   If there is no authority to overcome any anticipated barriers or obstacles then cooperation is required. Again this question must be addressed to enable performance improvement.

9. What new ideas or innovations could you offer?

   A final attempt to include any other ideas that the employee may have.

10. What boundaries or limitations are placed on your own performance?

    An opportunity for the employee to air any views they have on restrictions and constraints that they may perceive.

Appendix

TOOL 9: WHICH OF YOUR ACTIVITIES ADD THE MOST VALUE?

This Tool is very similar to any 'time management' diary system. The objective is to identify priorities, indicate where effort is expended and provide an assessment of which activities add the most value. It can be used in conjunction with Tool 8 above.

Perhaps try it out yourself first before asking any of your staff to complete the form.

How to complete the exercise

1. Divide all your activities into a few broad categories and list in column 1.
2. Put a figure in column 2 to indicate their relative importance (1 = most important; 5 = least important).
3. Indicate the percentage of your total time allocated to each of these activities in column 3.
4. In column 4 try to provide some indication of how this particular activity adds value and, if possible, an estimate of how much.

Activity	Importance (1–5)	% TIME	How it adds value and how much
Managing team of five people	1	10	Unable to quantify.
Administration	5	30	Basic administration and support only. Could improve admin. efficiency.
Quality assurance	2	10	Keeps customer returns close to zero. 1 return equals minimum cost of £1,000
Meetings	3	30	Only 10% of meetings worthwhile
Producing management information	4	20	New report on defects in goods inwards resulted in £20,000 credit from supplier.

So what do you now do with this information?

1. If you have many different categories of activity (say, as many as 10 or 12) does your role need a greater focus? Perhaps you have never really properly considered which activities fall into common categories.

2. If you genuinely believe that only 10 per cent of the meetings you attend are worthwhile then it might be worth keeping a diary of exactly which meetings are a waste of time and how long you spend in them. Your subjective views should be made more objective if you want to reduce the time you spend in pointless meetings.

3. Does the percentage of time spent on each activity match its importance? How can you only spend 10 per cent of your time working directly with your team when you regard it as a number one priority?

4. What about putting more thought into which of your activities could add the most value? Trying to put some £ signs on the effect of these activities may help you to prioritise your time and effort.

5. If you have ever been on a time management course, or know someone who has, have you ever wondered why it did not seem to have a lasting effect? What has to be put in place for this tool to bring about improved performance?

Appendix

TOOL 10: SPOT THE PERFORMANCE AND ADDED VALUE MEASURES

What is the difference between an activity measure, a performance measure and an added value measure? Activities tell us virtually nothing about performance and so produce useless data. Performance measures tell us enough to know what an improvement would look like. But performance says nothing about added value (*see* Chapter 8).

Look at the examples below and try to categorise them into activity, performance and added value measures. This tool is intended to sharpen up your thinking and reduce the number of measures you use.

a. Number of training days per employee
b. Output per employee
c. Average recruitment cost
d. Profit per employee
e. Personnel dept spend per employee
f. Calls handled per hour
g. Sales margin %
h. Sales visits per day
i. Sales volume (in units sold)
j. Staff turnover (e.g.15%)
k. Customer satisfaction survey
l. Rework hours
m. A level points per GCSE grade
n. Hospital bed usage (patients per bed, per annum)

Answers:

a. Pure activity. Did they learn anything?
b. Performance – but where is the corresponding cost/quality metric?
c. Activity – what about the quality of recruits? Should this measure go up or down?
d. Added value
e. Activity – who says they are doing anything useful?
f. Activity – could be a busy but ineffective little bee.
g. Added value – margin shows revenue relative to cost
h. Activity – great if the number of sales visits correlates with actual sales.
i. Performance – but what about cost of sales?
j. Activity – do you want 10 per cent or 20 per cent?
k. Performance and probably, hopefully, added value
l. Performance? – why not get rid of rework altogether?
m. Added value – compares outputs at age 18 to inputs at age 16
n. Activity – and let's check mortality and patient outcomes!

TOOL 11: PERFORMANCE TREND CHART

Name: .... **Date of birth:** ....

Rating period: From: To:	Company/division	Position	Rater 1	Rater 2	Comments and signature
1/6/95 31/12/95	XYZ Plastics	Supervisor	6	7	New appointment – developing into role well.
1/1/96 31/12/96	XYZ Plastics	Supervisor	8	8	Has matured in this role.
1/1/97 30/9/97	XYZ Polymers	Production Manager	8	8	Has made a good transition to management.
1/10/97 1/1/98	ABC	Senior Prod. Manager	7	7	Settled in very quickly.
1/1/98 1/4/98	ABC	Operations Manager	5	4	Some concerns at this stage about promotion.

Although this particular example is fictitious it is meant to illustrate a classic example of over-promotion. Whatever we might criticise this simple form for in terms of its lack of detail or sophistication, the aim is to produce a more reliable performance trend rather than a snapshot.

The trend here is of someone who developed well, accepting increasing responsibility. The assessment as Senior Production Manager was not as good as Production Manager. Here was a warning sign when considering further promotion.

This chart can be adapted in many ways. For example, it could contain some reference to value generated in each of these positions. Imagine how revealing a picture would be produced if this chart were kept up to date at one-, three- or six-monthly intervals over, say, ten years.

Appendix

TOOL 12: REDESIGNING THE ORGANISATION TO IMPROVE PERFORMANCE

Although organisation design can add a great deal of value it is not the simplest of tasks. We could write a book on this one subject alone so this tool should be regarded as a gentle introduction to the practicalities of organisation design.

Before you start:

- Please ensure you have read Chapter 13.

- Normally you will already have come to the conclusion that the existing process or structure is inefficient.

- Remember that the sole objective of this exercise is to improve employee and organisational performance

There are four steps to follow.

Step 1: Draw a process

First, draw a simple series of boxes with each step of a process. One is shown below for guidance. This is a list of the main steps when a customer rings up for some product information. Show, if possible, through which departments the process passes.

Customer enquiry process

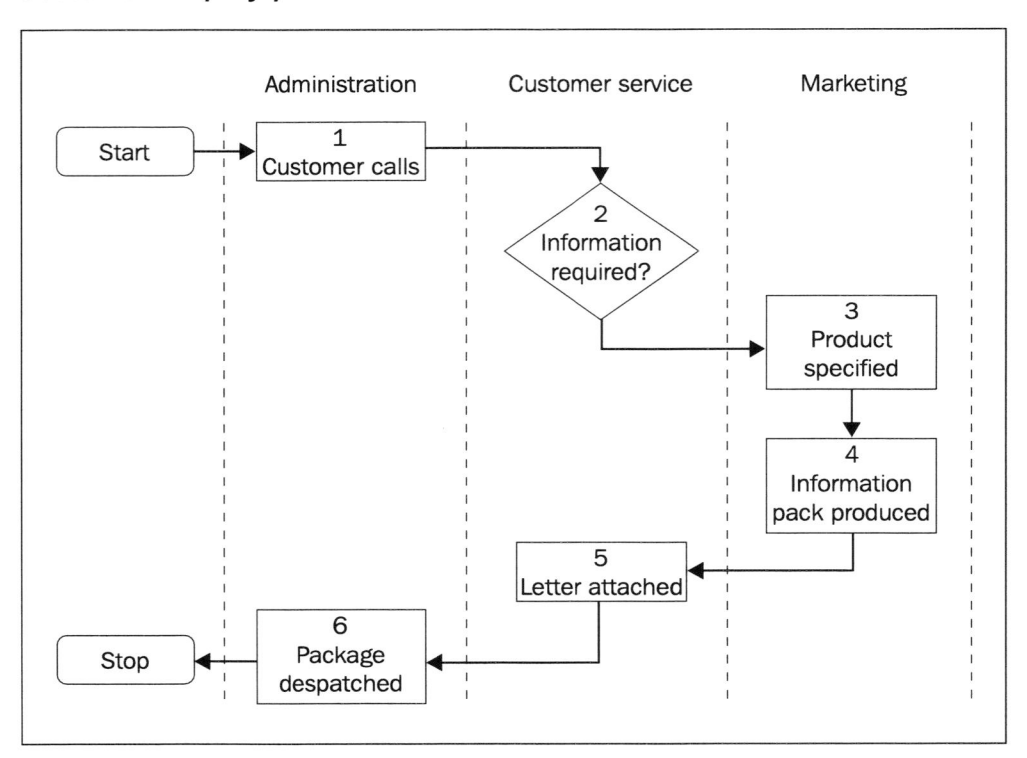

```
              Administration    Customer service    Marketing

  Start  →   1                       
             Customer calls    
                                  2
                                  Information
                                  required?
                                                         3
                                                         Product
                                                         specified

                                                         4
                                                         Information
                                                         pack produced

                                  5
                                  Letter attached
             6
             Package
  Stop  ←   despatched
```

Try to keep this first diagram as simple as possible. Often process flow diagrams become too complicated and unmanageable. The only other information on this diagram is the departments the enquiry passes through.

When drawing any process diagram always start with an output (the despatch of a product information package here). Then think where the process starts (a call). Then link the two by a series of boxes.

Now, at first glance, are there any ways in which the process itself could be improved? Why do marketing have to get involved in compiling basic product information? Why shouldn't the customer service team handle the whole process? Alternatively, why not have reception handle all of these calls?

Step 2: Identify the people in the process

The diagram above, as it stands, does not mention any people by name. So put at least one name against each of the boxes you produce.

In this example they are:

1. Deirdre the receptionist
2. Phil in customer service
3. Steve in marketing
4. Steve in marketing
5. Sue in customer service
6. Jim in the post room

Is each person fully trained and capable of carrying out their tasks?

Step 3: Collect some performance information

Try to attach measures to each of the following:

- How long does it take to undertake this process?
- Are there any delays or bottlenecks?
- Is each part of the process being correctly and efficiently carried out?
- How many errors are made?
- Do you have any customer feedback information (e.g. how long it takes to get some simple product information)?

Also, how much improvement could be made? Decide on a target. Who has to perform better and by how much?

Step 4: Consider where the people sit in the structure

Should anyone in the process be able to control any other part of the process? If customer service 'owns' this process can Phil control steps 3 to 6 to make sure it works well? Should Deirdre and/or Steve work in customer service?

TOOL 13: CHECKING LEVELS OF UNDERSTANDING

In Chapter 2 we looked at seven different levels of understanding. If you are reading this book in the sequence that was intended, then you will use this tool twice, at the beginning and when you have finished. If you have not made much progress in your understanding of employee performance measurement then reread the necessary sections.

Also, try to compile a list of questions which can check understanding of another topic (e.g. total quality, e-commerce, knowledge management, human capital, process re-engineering – the potential list is endless). It is especially interesting to use a questionnaire to check that there is a common level of understanding among senior managers and directors. If there is not, do not be surprised if new initiatives fail.

Use the simple list below to devise your own set of questions for a questionnaire. You may want a number of questions for each level. One-to-one interviews are the best way to undertake this survey, though. It will be more confidential, less threatening and, therefore, more revealing.

How well do you understand employee performance measurement?

- *Level 1 – Intuitive*

    Do you intuitively feel that employee measurement is necessary and worthwhile?

- *Level 2 – Knowledge*

    How much knowledge do you have on this subject? Have you ever seen a rating scale in an appraisal, for example? What do you know about performance related pay?

- *Level 3 – Principles (basic)*

    Do you know about baseline measures and how to collect them?

- *Level 4 – Application (simple)*

    Do you understand the principles well enough to produce a performance distribution curve?

- *Level 5 – Principles (advanced)*

    Have you made a connection between performance and learning? Do you understand the difference between performance and added value?

- *Level 6 – Adaptive*

    Would you be able to apply the principles in your team by inviting members of other teams to join you for a project to improve performance across the organisation?

Appendix

- *Level 7 – Innovative*

    Could you now devise some new ways of looking at performance and even generate some metrics that no one else has thought of? Would these ideas break down structural and hierarchical barriers?

References

Covey, Stephen (1990) *7 Habits of Highly Effective People*. Fireside.

Handy, Charles (1992) *Understanding Organisations*. Penguin.

Harrington, H. J. (1991) *Business Process Improvement*. McGraw-Hill.

Herzberg, Frederick (1993) *The Motivation to Work*. Transaction Publishing reprint.

Jaques, Elliott (1999) *Creativity and Work*. Canadian Center for Leadership and Strategy.

Kaplan, Robert S. and Norton, David P. (1996) *The Balanced Scorecard*. Harvard Business School.

Kearns, Paul (1995) *Measuring HR and the Impact on the Bottom Line*. Financial Times Management.

Kearns, Paul and Miller, Tony (1996) *Measuring the Impact of Training and Development on the Bottom Line*. Financial Times Management.

Kolb, D. A. (1984) *Experiential Learning: Experience as the Source of Learning and Development*. Prentice Hall.

Maslow, Abraham H. (1987) *Motivation and Personality*, 3rd edn. Addison-Wesley.

Peters, Tom and Waterman, Robert (1998) *In Search of Excellence*. Warner Books.

Schaffer, Robert H. and Thomson, Harvey J. (1992) 'Successful change programs begin with results', *Harvard Business Review*, January–February.

Senge, Peter *et al.* (1994) *The Fifth Discipline Fieldbook*. Nicholas Brealey.

Shewart, Walter (1929) *The Old Way*. Azusa Pacific University.